GOD'S
Master Plan
of
Salvation

BY PHILIP DELRE

VOICE PUBLISHING USA

God's Master Plan of Salvation

Originally published under the title: *Jesus Christ The Master Evangelist*

Published by Voice Publishing, a publishing ministry of Voice in the Wilderness Ministries.
Belvidere, IL 61008 USA

All Rights Reserved. Copyright © 2003

Updated in 2018

Scripture taken from the New King James Bible. Copyright ©1982 by Thomas Nelson, Inc. Used by permission. All rights reserved.

ISBN 0-9909318-3-8
ISBN 978-0-9909318-3-6

Printed in the United States of America.

*"If Christianity is not true, it is unimportant.
If it is true, nothing is more important."*
—C.S. Lewis

INTRODUCTION

When the Roman Empire ruled the world (with an iron first), it used all of its political and military power to try and stop Christianity from spreading. Meanwhile, the Apostles dedicated themselves to prayer and the ministry of the Word. Armed with the Gospel, inflamed with the love of Christ, and undaunted by the power of Rome, they turned the world upside down!

So, what made the first century church willing to be burned at the stake, boiled in oil, fed to the lions, and crucified rather than deny Christ? They knew God's master plan of salvation – personally!

I enjoy the art and science of defending the Christian faith, an academic discipline known as apologetics. The latest discoveries from science, archeology, etc., are wonderful for the edification and the building up of God's people. These intellectual arguments can play a role in helping those who have legitimate questions and concerns about Christianity.

Furthermore, I believe it would be wonderful if God's people were all well-versed in: Theology, Hebrew and Greek grammar, Bible interpretation, Bible prophecy, church history, comparative religion, archaeology, philosophy, creation science, logic, and debate! However, none of these academic disciplines (as wonderful as they are) has an ounce of power to convict a man of sin, which is what Jesus came to save us from (Matt. 1:21).

When it comes to presenting the plan of salvation to others, God left us a perfect, systematic theology of evangelism that cannot be improved upon by any man. In fact, there is one argument more compelling than someone you know coming back from the dead to tell you what's on the other side! Read this book carefully and you'll find it.

This project is a humble attempt to help my fellow man understand God's master plan of salvation and be able to explain it to others, "Not according to the wisdom of man's words, but in demonstration of the Spirit's power" (1 Cor. 2:4).

Since neither God nor His Word has changed, the Gospel is still the power of God (Rom. 1:16). Join me in studying the greatest truth ever known to man, in the light and fire of God's holy Word.

TABLE OF CONTENTS

1. **THE MOST AWESOME DEMONSTRATION OF POWER ANYONE HAS EVER SEEN** 7
   Of all the miracles in the Bible, three are in a class by themselves, and all three contain a clear message from God–for you!

2. **THE BIBLE'S BIG PICTURE** 15
   Understanding the relationship between the Old and the New Testament will add light years to your understanding of God's Word!

3. **THE LAW OF GOD IS WRITTEN ON EVERY MAN'S HEART** 25
   No man will stand before God with any excuse for ignoring or denying Him. Find out why in this chapter.

4. **GOD'S MASTER PLAN OF SALVATION** 33
   Unveiling a mystery that has baffled thinking people for centuries!

5. **HOW TO PRESENT THE GOSPEL THE WAY JESUS DID** 43
   "I have been in church all my life, and never really understood the Gospel until today. Thank You!"

6. **IS THIS REALLY NEW TESTAMENT THEOLOGY?** 51
   A close look at law in the New Testament by an imaginary court.

7. **DON'T TAKE MY WORD FOR IT** 65
   Quotes from the greatest minds in the history of the church who understood and applied God's most compelling argument.

8. **THE PERFECT LAW OF LIBERTY** 75
   When God says "No" to one thing, He is saying "Yes" to living the abundant life Jesus speaks of.

9. **IF GOD IS GOOD, WHY IS THERE SO MUCH EVIL IN THE WORLD?** 89
   The answer will blow you away.

10. **THE FEAR OF MAN VS. THE FEAR OF GOD** 97
    This sermon was recorded at a three thousand member church and we had 940 requests for copies of the message!

11. **APPENDIX ONE: BUT WE'RE NOT UNDER LAW, WE'RE UNDER GRACE** 111
    Clarifying some misunderstood verses in the New Testament.

12. **APPENDIX TWO: SATAN'S MASTER PLAN OF EVANGELISM AND THE IMMORAL MAJORITY** 121

CHAPTER ONE

THE MOST AWESOME DEMONSTRATION OF POWER ANYONE HAS EVER SEEN

In northwestern Saudi Arabia, out in the middle of the desert, and surrounded by oceans of sand, there is a small "top secret" military outpost. A handful of Saudi marksmen armed with automatic weapons and guard dogs patrol an area surrounded by a chain-link fence. Their mission? To keep any and all curiosity seekers away from this site.

In addition to the military patrol (remember this is in the middle of nowhere), there is a large sign posted in front of the guard house, outside the fence, carrying this warning in Arabic and in English,

This is a protected archeological site

All trespassers will be prosecuted

So, what's behind the fence that the Saudi government does not want the world to see? Shrouded in secrecy, is an 8,465 foot mountain known to the local Bedouins as Jabal Musa. You can find it on a good map under the name Jabal Al Lawz.

So why would anyone want to "protect" a mountain out in the middle of the desert? If the truth was known and if the Saudis allowed people to examine this area, Biblical scholars, archeologists, and journalists would hail this as one of, if not the greatest archeological discovery of all time.

What happened here is so significant, and the evidence is so compelling, if word got out, many people would be willing to risk their lives by sneaking into the country to see this incredible discovery. Some already have, and *that* is why the area is guarded.

Since the Saudis' preferred method of dealing with "infidels" is beheading, the potential to create *another* international crisis similar to the fight for sovereignty over the Temple Mount in Jerusalem is real!

WHAT IS SO UNUSUAL ABOUT THIS MOUNTAIN?

At the base of the mountain, there is a huge formation of boulders (some weighing hundreds of tons) carefully placed on top of one another three stories high, a hundred feet across, and flat on top.

This engineering feat required a large number of people who were *highly motivated* and had a good deal of experience moving stones of this magnitude.

Whoever it was that went to all this trouble, also had a fetish for cattle. Etched into the sides of this giant memorial are pictures of cows and bulls. Strange indeed, since cattle have never been indigenous to the desert.

In addition, there are large piles of smaller rocks every four hundred yards, forming a semi circle around the mountain. They appear to serve as boundary markers, as if to say, "This far and no farther."

At the foot of the mountain there is a v-shaped pit, with carefully placed stones along the sides to form walls. It is believed that this area was used for animal sacrifice. Next to that, there are twelve hand-hewn pillars made of stone, representing a memorial to something very significant to someone. The question is, who?

Most unusual of all is the fact that the mountain itself (made of solid granite rock) is brown, but the peek (the top third of the mountain) is shiny black. It appears as if the top of the mountain had been exposed to an intense heat and melted by a giant incinerator!

Scholars and archeologists who have examined the evidence on and around this mountain (based on eye witness accounts, pictures, and video tape smuggled out of the country), believe this may be the actual site where God gave Moses the Ten Commandments! All of the evidence matches perfectly with the Biblical account of the Israelites exodus from Egypt.

Providentially, it only rains a fraction of an inch every ten years in this area, so all the effects left by God, and two to three million Israelites, have been perfectly preserved for thousands of years. There are a number of great books and videos documenting the facts of this discovery that are nothing short of spectacular![1]

THE MOST POWERFUL SERMON EVER PREACHED

The following is the biblical account of what happened at Mt. Sinai. This is one of, if not the most powerful and pertinent stories in all the Bible. It's found in Exodus 19:16 - 20:19. This is awesome!

> *So it came about on the third day, when it was morning, that there were thunder and lightning flashes and a thick cloud upon the mountain and a very loud trumpet sound, so that all the people who were in the camp trembled.*
>
> *And Moses brought the people out of the camp to meet God, and they stood at the foot of the mountain. Now Mount Sinai was all in smoke because the LORD descended upon it in fire; and its smoke ascended like the smoke of a furnace, and the whole mountain quaked violently.*
>
> *When the sound of the trumpet grew louder and louder, Moses spoke and God answered him with thunder. And the LORD came down on Mount Sinai, to the top of the mountain.*
>
> *Then God spoke all these words, saying, I am the LORD your God, who brought you out of the land of Egypt, out of the house of slavery.*
>
> 1. *Thou shalt have no other gods before Me.*
> 2. *Thou shalt not make for yourself an idol.*
> 3. *Thou shalt not take the name of the LORD in vain.*
> 4. *Remember the Sabbath day, to keep it holy.*
> 5. *Honor your father and your mother.*
> 6. *Thou shalt not murder.*
> 7. *Thou shalt not commit adultery.*
> 8. *Thou shalt not steal.*
> 9. *Thou shalt not lie.*
> 10. *Thou shalt not covet against thy neighbor.*

IT IS IMPOSSIBLE TO OVERSTATE THE THEOLOGICAL AND THE PRACTICAL SIGNIFICANCE OF GOD'S MESSAGE FROM MOUNT SINAI.

When the Supreme Commander of the universe decended on Mt. Sinai, He was preceeded by an entourage of sight and sound that was so dreadful, so utterly terrifying, when it was over, the people begged Moses never to let God speak to them directly again. They were convinced one more manifestation of that magnitude would literally kill them. Here is the text from Ex. 20:19,

> *Then they said to Moses, "You speak with us, and we will hear; but let not God speak with us, lest we die."*

Herbert Lockyer in his book, *All the Miracles of the Bible*, speaking of God's revelation at Mt. Sinai, wrote,

> . . . there has never been so awful a manifestation...at any other place or time, nor will be until the endtime period of human history. [2]

This raises a most important and fundamental question: Why would a loving God do such a thing to His own people? What was the point in almost scaring them to death with this demonstration of power? The answer is found at the end of the story,

> *And Moses said to the people, "Do not be afraid; for God has come in order to test you, and in order that the fear of Him may remain with you, so that you may not sin" (Ex. 20:20).*

WHAT DOES ALL THIS HAVE TO DO WITH YOU? EVERYTHING—KEEP READING!

One question people often ask is, "How did we get the Bible?" In 2 Peter 1:21 we are told: "For no prophecy was ever made by an act of human will, but men moved by the Holy Spirit spoke from God." But, there is one part of the Bible, utterly unique, unlike any other.

While there are many miracles recorded in Scripture, three are in a class by themselves: Only creation and the incarnation of Christ (His deity, virgin birth, death and resurrection), compare in terms of power, glory and significance to God's revelation at Mt. Sinai. Consider the following facts.

Scripture reveals that God has communicated with us in many ways. They include: Creation, the Bible, Jesus Christ, the Holy Spirit, prophets, apostles, angels, and even a donkey! He revealed His will through dreams, visions, and the mysterious *Urim* and *Thummim*, described in Numbers 27:21. But, when it came to the Ten Commandments, Ex. 20:1 says, "And God spoke all these words."

The giving of the Ten Commandments represents the one and only time God the Father descended to Earth in His omnipotent state and spoke audibly to the *entire* nation of Israel.

The Ten Commandments are the one and only part of the Bible God personally wrote with His own "finger," and etched them in *stone*! Exodus 31:18,

> And when He had finished speaking with him upon Mount Sinai, He gave Moses the two tablets of the testimony, tablets of stone, written by the finger of God.

GOD'S EMPHASIS ON THE MORAL LAW DOES NOT END THERE— IT BEGINS THERE.

God instructed His people to build a Tabernacle, and later Solomon's Temple. The focal point of each was the inner sanctum called the Holy of Holies. And, what was inside the most holy place? The Ark of the Covenant containing the Ten Commandments!

The Ark of God (one of three "Arks" in the Bible) was a rectangular box approximately 4 feet by 2.5 feet, made of acacia wood, and overlaid with pure gold. The lid of the Ark, called the "Mercy Seat," was solid gold. On top of the Mercy Seat were two Cherubim (angels) facing each other, looking down, with outstretched wings.

Once a year on the Day of Atonement, God's divine presence (called the Shekhina glory) would appear between the Cherbim, enthroned on the Mercy Seat. The high priest would then sprinkle the blood of a perfect sacrifice, prefiguring the work of Christ. The sins of the people were declared "paid in full" on the basis of a substitute.

HOW DO YOU RECONCILE JUSTICE AND MERCY WITHOUT COMPROMISING ONE OR THE OTHER?

The Ark of the Covenant (covenant means: a binding contract, a pledge, a commitment, a guarantee), served as an object lesson to show us how a perfecly holy and just God (He must punish sin or He would be unjust) can forgive a perfectly guilty person without compromising His justice! Since the penalty for sin is death, in order for a savior to save you, he would have to be sinless and die for you. That is exactly what Jesus did on the cross.

It is Mt. Sinai that gives Jesus' sacrifice it's literal, historical and theological context. As we shall see in the chapters that follow, the New Testament teaches us that the Ten Commandments define what constitutes sin. How important is that?

- It is sin that seperates us from God (Isa. 59:2)
- It is sin that Jesus came to save us from (Matt. 1:21)
- It is sin that necessitated Christs' death, and served as the payment for our sin (Rom. 4:25)

RUNNING TO WIN

From the time I was old enough to run, all the way through school, I never lost a running race. Every year in school when they posted the names and the times for the 50-yard dash, I was number one. Even at my dad's company picnics I won every race, every year.

When I was in eighth grade, however, I ran into a little technical problem. When it came time to run the dash that year, my name was called, I came up to the line, the gun went off, the clock started, and I took off like lightning.

About halfway through the race, however, the eighth grade girls' class came filing out behind me. It seems a couple of them yelled out, "Go! Go!" and I made the mistake of looking back to see who it was. That look cost me two seconds!

As soon as the coach told me my time, I said, "Coach, you saw what happened. You know I can do better than that. Please let me run it again."

His "No" was final. I was posted in second place that year. As you can see, I still haven't gotten over it!

Fact: The shortest distance between two points is a straight line. If you even look to the right or to the left, not only will it cost you; you may even lose the race. Remember Lot's wife?

If you want to run the race to win the soul-winner's crown, do not look to the right or to the left. God's moral law is the straightest line and the shortest distance to the Gospel you will ever find. If you're not convinced of that, keep reading, there's a lot more to learn about the Ten Commandments. So, get out your New Testament, and let's take a ride. We're gonna have some fun!

SMALL GROUP DISCUSSION QUESTIONS FOR CHAPTER ONE

1. How are the unsaved characterized in Romans 3:11-18?
2. In terms of how the Bible was written (see 2 Peter 1:21), how are the Ten Commandments different?
3. How is that significant?
4. What does "etched in stone" symbolize?
5. List each commandment one at a time and answer the question: What would happen to our world if everyone obeyed this commandment?
6. Were the 10 commandments given before or after the Israelites were redeemed from Egyptian slavery? What is the significance of this fact?
7. How can the fear of God be positive?
8. What did you learn from this chapter?
9. If you knew for a fact that Jesus would return in one year, what would you do differently?
10. What does God want to save you from? Compare your answer to:Matt. 1:21, Rom. 5:8-10 and Rev. 21:8.

CHAPTER TWO

THE BIBLE'S BIG PICTURE

Understanding the relationship that exists between the Old and the New Testament will add light years to your understanding of God and His Word. Context is king in determining what the Bible means by what it says.

UNDERSTANDING THE RELATIONSHIP BETWEEN LAW AND GRACE IS ESSENTIAL TO UNDERSTANDING THE GOSPEL.

The Old Testament is commonly referred to as "The law," and the New Testament is known conceptually as "The Gospel of grace." To be sure, grace is found in the Old Testament (Gen. 15:6 for example), and law in the New. If you are not sure of that, hangeth thou in there brethren and I wilt showeth thee.

The predominant themes respectively are: law in the Old, grace in the New, in that order and for good reason. Simply stated, it is because we have broken God's law that we need His grace. Grace presupposes law. The importance of understanding these two foundational Biblical principles and their relationship to each other *cannot be overstated*.

As much as I hate to mention his name, the first time Satan is sighted in Scripture is right in the beginning of both the Old and the New Testaments (Gen.3 and Matt.4). In both cases he is taking God's word out of context. This mistake can be fatal, and is to this day, one of the leading causes of false doctrine and division in the church.

> *And no wonder, for even Satan transforms himself into an angel of light. Therefore it is not surprising if his ministers also transform themselves into ministers of righteousness; whose end shall be according to their deeds (2 Cor. 11:14-15).*

Do you understand the implications of that verse? There are ministers, who stand in pulpits, who quote from the Bible (taking it out of context) who are actually serving Satan's agenda! Sometime around the turn of the 19th century the enemy came in like a flood, and liberalism established a beachhead in many mainline denominational seminaries. In the spiritual battle that ensued, the prevailing wind of doctrine was, since the church age began in Acts chapter two, everything prior to that is Old Testament law. And, since Christ "fulfilled" the law (more on that in Appendix One), the Old Testament is practically obsolete, and serves only as history. This doctrine in effect, removes the entire New Testament from its context! Nothing could be further from the truth.

THE VERY FIRST VERSE IN THE NEW TESTAMENT FORCES YOU BACK TO THE OLD TESTAMENT.

This is the record of the genealogy of Jesus Christ the Son of David, the Son of Abraham (Matt. 1:1).

Matthew 1:1 shows us two things. First, that God always keeps His promises, and second, that the Bible is one book. This verse says in effect, "If you are starting here, you have to go back to Genesis, brother!" Who would pick up any other book and start reading in the middle? Yet, people do that with the Bible and wonder why they have trouble understanding it.

> Starting in Matthew is like walking into a movie half-way through. It's like thinking you are telling a good joke when all you can remember is the punch line.

Without understanding the covenant promises that God made with Abraham and David, Matt. 1:1 would be utterly boring, yet to those who understand it in the context of Genesis 12, this verse explodes with excitement. This same principle holds true for more than 1,200 verses in the New Testament!

What is the significance of Christ dying on Passover and being raised on the Jewish festival of First Fruits were it not for the book of Exodus? What sense would John have made when he said of Jesus, "Behold the Lamb of God who takes away the sin of the world," or when Jesus said, "This is the new covenant in My blood," were it not for the doctrine of the blood atonement in Leviticus?

Most of us think of Matthew as the first book of the New Testament, and it is. Matthew is *also* the 40th book of the 66 that make up the Bible. The number 40 is significant since throughout Scripture, it represents the number of completion.

Furthermore, the Old Testament contains truths that are essential for a proper worldview and are found in no other source. For example, only in the book of Genesis (which means origin) do we discover the origin of the universe; of man and his fall into sin; the doctrine of marriage and the family; the establishment of the nations, languages; and the prophetic significance of Israel!

Only in the Old Testament are we told of the rebellion in Heaven that turned Lucifer into Satan, and thus the origin of evil and the promise of a Savior.

> The Old Testament worldview is clearly distinct from other worldviews, such as polytheism, pantheism, gnosticism, deism, atheism, and naturalism. The New Testament does not provide another worldview but simply assumes the one taught in the Old Testament. [1]

JUST TO MAKE SURE NO ONE COULD EVER CLAIM THE BIBLE WAS A MAN-MADE CONSPIRACY, GOD PUT 400 YEARS OF SILENCE BETWEEN THE TESTAMENTS!

The Old Testament is the foundation upon which the New Testament is built, and the New Testament constantly refers back to the Old to establish its validity. Through fulfilled prophecy, each continuously points back and forth to the other as proof positive of its divine authenticity and its perfect unity.

Without the New Testament, the Old Testament would be incomplete, and without the Old Testament, the New Testament would be utterly incomprehensible. Each is a guide to properly understanding the other.

According to Malachi 3:6 the Lord does not change. For God to change, He would either have to get better or worse, that's impossible; He is perfect! Likewise, according to the New Testament God's definition of *sin* has never changed either. 1 John 3:4 says,

> *Whosoever commits sin transgresses the law: for sin is the transgression of the law (KJV).*

THE BOOK OF ROMANS

And, *what* law is John referring to? The answer is found in the book written by the "Apostle to the Gentiles" and addressed to the Christians at Rome. Romans was written *after* the church age began (in Acts chapter two).

The book of Romans is considered by theologians to be the greatest treatise on the doctrine of *salvation by grace* in all of Scripture. Martin Luther's commentary on the book begins with these words,

> This epistle is really the chief part of the New Testament and the very purest Gospel.

So, what does the chief part of the New Testament and the very purest Gospel have to say about the law? Beginning in Romans 2:14,

> *for when Gentiles, who do not have the law, by nature do the things in the law, these, although not having the law, are a law to themselves, who show the work of the law written in their hearts, their conscience also bearing witness.*

> *because by the works of the Law no flesh will be justified in His sight; for through the Law comes the knowledge of sin (Rom. 3:20).*

> *Do we then nullify the Law through faith? May it never be! On the contrary, we establish the Law (Rom. 3:31).*

> *What shall we say then? Is the Law sin? May it never be! On the contrary, I would not have come to know sin except through the Law; for I would not have known about coveting if the Law had not said, "You shall not covet" (Rom. 7:7).*

Romans 7:7 leaves no doubt that Paul is referring to the moral law as contained in the Ten Commandments. Therefore, we can *paraphrase* Romans 3:20 this way,

> by the works of the law no one will be justified in His sight; for *through the Ten Commandments comes the knowledge of sin!*

Romans 3:31 proves beyond the shadow of doubt that the moral law has not been abolished by the coming of Christ, as some have claimed. And, Romans 7:7 shows us that sin is still defined by the Ten Commandments.

THE LAW OF LOVE

One of the most strategic pieces of spiritual real estate temporarily controlled by the enemy is the idea that law and love are opposing forces. Since love is the greatest gift, and God Himself is love, and since love endures forever, no one would dare be opposed to love, right? Therefore, whatever opposes love must be evil and done away with.

Unfortunately, this is how the law is perceived by many people. This understanding is completely erroneous. The moral law is divided into two "tables." The first four are vertical, and teach us how to love God. The next six are horizontal, and teach us how to love our fellow man. In the following Scripture, Jesus uses the words *law* and *love* in the same breath! Here is how He summarized the Ten Commandments,

> *Teacher, which is the greatest commandment in the Law? Jesus replied: "Love the Lord your God with all your heart and with all your soul and with all your mind. This is the first and greatest commandment. And the second is like it: Love your neighbor as yourself. All the Law and the Prophets hang on these two commandments" (Matthew 22:36–40).*

Rather than being mutually exclusive, law and love are mutually affinitive. The Ten Commandments show us how to express our love for God and for our neighbor in a tangible way. See for yourself,

> *Owe nothing to anyone except to love one another; for he who loves his neighbor has fulfilled the Law. For this, "You shall not commit adultery, you shall not murder, you shall not steal, you shall not covet," and if there is any other commandment, it is summed up in this saying, "you shall love your neighbor as yourself." Love does no wrong to a neighbor; love therefore is the fulfillment of the Law" (Rom.13:8–10).*

Thanks to the moral law, *love* can actually be weighed and measured against an objective standard. Without the guidelines of the law, love would be abstract and relative. In 1 Cor. 13, we see the *effects* of love, whereas the moral law defines its *boundaries*.

In His infinite wisdom, God tells us that "love is the fulfillment of the law" (Rom. 13:10b). If I truly love my neighbor, according to Romans 13, I will:

- Honor his marriage covenant, and mine, by not lusting after his wife.
- I will forgive him when he wrongs me, rather than committing murder.
- I will honor his property by not stealing it.
- I will tell him the truth (and what truth is) when I speak to him.
- I will rejoice in the blessings God has given him, rather than coveting his goods.

Isn't that the kind of neighborhood in which you want to live? Can you even begin to imagine what would happen to our world if we all "kept the law" according to this standard?

The ability to define sin is the ability to define exactly why a person needs Jesus Christ (Matt. 1:21). Rather than telling a person he is a sinner, just tell him what sin is, and watch the Holy Spirit do what only He can (John 16:8)! The power of Sinai has never diminished. I know of nothing more exhilarating than leading someone to Christ.

Jesus summed up the law this way in Matthew 5:17-19,

> *Do not think that I came to abolish the law or the Prophets; I did not come to abolish, but to fulfill. For assuredly, I say to you, until heaven and Earth pass away, one jot or one tittle will by no means pass from the law until all is fulfilled.*
>
> *Whoever then annuls one of the least of these commandments, and so teaches others, shall be called least in the kingdom of heaven; but who ever keeps and teaches them, he shall be called great in the kingdom of heaven.*

MANY PEOPLE EQUATE LAW WITH LEGALISM, AND SEE GRACE AS A WILDCARD YOU CAN PLAY ANYTIME YOU DON'T LIKE THE RULES!

In 1855, Charles Haddon Spurgeon, one of the finest minds in the history of the church, said,

> *There is no point upon which men make greater mistakes than upon the relation that exists between the law and the Gospel.*

Even though the Old Testament comprises 70% of the Bible, the word "law" appears more times in the New Testament than in the Old.

Satan's campaign to distort the *legitimate* use of the law has been so successful, many Christian leaders and their congregations are scared to death of the word. The fear of being labeled a "legalist" is a powerful weapon in the hands of the enemy. Christian leaders can talk about holiness and obedience, as long as they do not use the word "law." One wonders, then, what it is we are supposed to obey, and what constitutes *practical* holiness.

Part of the reason for all the confusion is because the New Testament "appears" to contradict itself on this issue. The confusion is easily cleared up when we pay close attention to context.

WE MUST DISTINGUISH BETWEEN THE CIVIL, THE CEREMONIAL, AND THE MORAL LAW.

Altogether, there are 613 laws that constitute Old Testament Judaism. To clarify our understanding of how the law applies to the church, we must define our terms.

- The civil law was was designed to be enforced by the government of ancient Israel.
- The ceremonial law, which had to do with the Jewish religion of feasts, fasts, and the sacrificial system.
- The moral law, as contained in the Ten Commandments.

The civil law has no application for the 21st century Christians, since we are not citizens living under the government of ancient Israel.

The ceremonial law (which included the sacrificing of animals) were prophetic road-signs pointing us to Christ. They provide 1,500 years of literal, historical, and theological context so when John the Baptist saw Jesus and said, "Behold the Lamb of God who takes away the sin of the world," His atoning death would make perfect sense.

The ceremonial laws were fulfilled literally, legally, prophetically, and spiritually when Jesus, the sinless Lamb of God, was sacrificed on the cross, "once *and* for all" (Heb. 7:27; 9:12, 1 Pet. 3:18). As a result, we are no longer living under the dispensation of the Old Testament ceremonial law.

The moral law defines sin. The *definition* of sin (something God is still opposed to) has never changed (Rom. 3:20; 31, 7:7). Therein lies the problem and the solution to the confusion about "law" in the New Testament.

CHRIST IS STILL BETWEEN TWO THIEVES

So, how is it that we have come so far in losing the proper concept of the moral law? Here is how it was done. Since we are saved by grace alone, and, since the New Testament says Christ fulfilled the law, all law became equated with legalism. Legalism is heresy, heresy is false doctrine, and false doctrine is the work of the enemy.

The result of this misunderstanding means Christ is still in between two thieves—antinomianism on one side, and legalism on the other. Both are equally deadly, and both are prevalent to one degree or another in the church.

Legalism is the idea that you can add something to or subtract something from your salvation by what you do or don't do. This stands in direct opposition to God's grace.

Antinomianism means *no law*. This is the idea that there is no law whatsoever in the New Testament. All things are lawful as long as my conscience is clear and I live by love (as I define it).

As long as moral truth is considered relative, there is no chance for people to see their need of salvation. What would happen if the bricklayer abandoned the use of the square, the level, and the plumb? What if he decided that what is straight to you is not necessarily straight to him? His buildings would lack structural integrity and would soon collapse as a result.

Do you see why the devil hates the law and wants to destroy it?

Keep Reading

SMALL GROUP DISCUSSION QUESTIONS
FOR CHAPTER TWO

1. Compare Matt. 1:1 to Genesis 22:18 and Isa. 9:6-7. What is the significance of this connection?
2. What is legalism?
3. Give an example of legalism?
4. What is antinomianism?
5. Give an an example of antinomianism.
6. What are the effects of antinomianism in the church today?
7. What are the three categories of law in the Old Testament?
8. Who did Jesus say would be called great in the kingdom of heaven? Why?
9. According to Matt. 22:36-40 and Rom. 13:8-10, how are love and law related?
10. What is the relationship between law and grace? Compare Gal. 3:24 to Rom. 6:1 for help.

CHAPTER THREE

THE LAW OF GOD IS WRITTEN ON EVERY MAN'S HEART

I received a call one day from an organization known as Inner City Impact in Chicago. The man asked me if I would be interested in addressing their youth group at a weekend retreat. I said,

"I would love to address your youth group. What would you like me to teach on?"

The answer was, "Sexual purity." I gulped, and asked what age group they were and the answer was, "High school."

My heart sank as I hung up the phone. I remember thinking to myself, *I would much rather be locked up in a maximum security prison and preach on the love of God, rather than face these young people, and try to convince them that purity is the best way to go.*

Please don't misunderstand. I believe with all my heart that this is one of the most critical issues of our day, and it needs to be addressed. My problem was, I had never preached on that particular subject to that particular age group before, and I don't like to preach unless I have something compelling to say.

At the retreat, I had approximately 50 girls on my left, and 50 boys on my right. I asked the girls, "How would you like to know the three secrets that will make you the most eligible girl in your entire neighborhood for marriage?"

I was met with a resounding "Yes!"

I said, "A real man, a good man, will be looking for three things in a wife: someone he can respect, someone who is special, and someone who is a challenge. Now watch and listen very carefully."

I walked over to the boys and said, "Gentleman, if you had the opportunity to marry one of two women, both equally beautiful, both are equally talented, both are equally gifted, and both of them have dynamic personalities; in fact, they're identical twins. The only difference between the two is, one of them has had multiple sexual partners, and the other one is a virgin. How many will take the virgin? Raise your hands."

Without hesitation, *all of them* smiled and raised their hands. I said, "Gentleman, keep your hands right where they are!" I walked back over to the girls and said,

"Ladies, I don't care what they're telling you in the back seat of the car on Saturday night, take a good look at 'em now, because there's the naked truth!"

I could see many of them turning their heads like curious puppies, obviously thinking to themselves, "Wow, there's a revolutionary concept. I never thought of that before."

I went on to say, "For those of you who are still virgins, just remember that you can always become like the girls who are not, but they can never become like you. As for those who have lost their virginity, I have some good news for you. It's never too late to start living right. The next best thing is 'secondary virginity.'

"You can decide today to remain celibate. If you have to wait one, two, five, or ten years for the right man to come along, and you tell him you have been waiting for him all that time, I guarantee you he will think you are someone he can respect; you are special; and you are a challenge." They *all* applauded![1]

ABSOLUTE TRUTH

Contrary to those who claim there is no such thing as absolute truth (which apparently is the only thing that is absolutely true), we live in a moral universe with an absolute standard of right and wrong.

Every man, from the beginning of time until the end of the world, whether or not he has ever read a Bible or even heard of Jesus Christ, knows in his *heart* it's wrong to murder, it's wrong to steal, it's wrong to lie, and it's wrong to have another man's wife. He knows it "instinctively." Whether he will admit it or not, that's another story. Which brings me to...

THE ATHEIST AND HIS CONSCIENCE

The so-called "intellectual" and finally, an "honest atheist," Aldus Huxley speaks for all atheists (whether they like it or not) in this priceless quote,

> I had motives for not wanting the world to have meaning; consequently assumed it had none, and was able without any difficulty to find satisfying reasons for this assumption . . . The philosopher who finds no meaning in the world is not concerned exclusively with a problem of pure metaphysics; he is also concerned to prove there is no valid reason why he personally should not do as he wants to do. For myself, as no doubt for most of my contemporaries, the philosophy of meaninglessness was essentially an instrument of liberation. The liberation we desired was simultaneously liberation from a certain political and economic system, and liberation from a certain system of morality. We objected to the morality because it interfered with our sexual freeom.[2]

ATHEISTS AREN'T BORN–THEY EVOLVE

A study was done a while back into all the famous atheists of history: Sartre, Kamoo, Nietzche, Freud, Marx, Madalyn Murray O'Hair, all the famous atheists of history, and every single one of them had something in common. They either lost their father when they were young, their father abandoned their family, or they had a terrible relationship with their father. That is very interesting because often these doubts aren't really driven by intellectual questions, they are being driven by an emotional issue that really blocks them from *wanting* to relate to a heavenly father because they feel so abandoned, or cheated, or hurt by their Earthly father.[3]

There you have it. Most of the time, the intellectual concerns people raise when they encounter the claims of Christ are only smoke screens (fig leaves) to cover the real issues, which are moral. Men love darkness rather than the light, and do not want to relinquish authority of their lives to God.

When all is said and done, if a person rejects Christianity, ultimately, it is the will *not the intellect* that stands in the way. Otherwise, God would be unjust in punishing unbelievers. Jesus said,

> *If any man is willing to do His will, he shall know of the teaching, whether it is of God, or whether I speak from Myself (Jn. 7:17). Also see Matt. 23:37.*

According to Rom. 1:18-20, *no one* will stand before God with *any excuse* for ignoring or denying Him,

> *For the wrath of God is revealed from heaven against all ungodliness and unrighteousness of men, who suppress the truth in unrighteousness, because that which is known about God is evident within them; for God made it evident to them. For since the creation of the world His invisible atributes, His eternal power and divine nature, have been clearly seen, being understood through what has been made, so that they are without excuse.*

In other words, all an honest person has to do is to take a good look at the sun, the moon, and the stars to *know*, that anything so complex, so perfectly designed and well balanced as is our world, and our universe, could in no way have made itself, and only "The fool says in his heart, there is no God" (Ps. 14:1).

This however, is only the general revelation that God exists. There is a huge difference between believing *in* God, and *believing* God! Intellectual ascent is not saving faith. Many people are intellectually convinced the Bible is true, yet continue to live as heathens!

> *Not everyone who says to Me, "Lord, Lord," will enter the kingdom of heaven; but he who does the will of My Father who is in heaven. Many will say to Me on that day, "Lord, Lord, did we not prophesy in Your name, and in Your name cast out demons, and in Your name perform many miracles?" And then I will declare to them, "I never knew you; depart from Me, you who practice lawlessness" (Matt. 7:21-23).*

THE POWER OF THE MORAL ARGUMENT

I personally enjoy the art and the science of defending the Christian faith known as apologetics. The latest discoveries from science, for example, are wonderful for the edification and the building up of the saints. Certainly these intellectual arguments can and do play a part in helping those who have *legitimate* questions and concerns about Christianity.

Furthermore, I do believe it would be wonderful if we were all well versed in: Theology, Hebrew and Greek grammar, Bible interpretation, Bible prophecy, church history, comparative religion, archeology, philosophy, creation science, logic, and debate! However, none of these academic disciplines (as wonderful as they are) has an ounce of power to convict a man of sin, which is, after all, the real issue. Sin is what Jesus came to save us from (Matt. 1:21).

SPIRITUAL TRUTH TRANSCENDS THE HUMAN INTELLECT

The truth of God's Word is *not* something the human intellect can analyze and synthesize apart from divine intervention by the Holy Spirit. Only He can open a man's heart *and mind* to "see" the glory of the Gospel. The book of First Corinthians, chapter two, is crystal clear,

> *This is what we speak, not in words taught us by human wisdom but in words taught by the Spirit, expressing spiritual truths in spiritual words. But the natural man receiveth not the things of the Spirit of God: for they are foolishness unto him: neither can he know them, because they are spiritually discerned (1 Cor. 2:14-17).*

So, if I want to communicate spiritual truth to a worldly wise man who is incapable of understanding it, how do I reach him? Man knows instictively (weather he will admit it or not) the difference between right and wrong. God's law is written in his heart. Romans 2:14-15,

> *For when Gentiles who do not have the Law do instinctively the things of the Law . . . they show the work of the Law written in their hearts, their conscience bearing witness, and their thoughts alternately accusing or else defending them.*

THERE IS THE CONTACT POINT BETWEEN GOD AND MAN

All of the scientific, philosophical, and legal arguments combined, offered by the most able orator, do not have an ounce of power to convict a man of sin. When it comes to communicating the Gospel a child armed with the moral law, is greater than the mightiest Ph.D. without it.

In John 16:8, we learn that the Holy Spirit's ministry is to "convict the world of sin, righteousness, and judgment." The word *convict* in the original Greek literally means:

- To show or prove one of wrong
- To expose the hidden things
- To correct or chastise in a moral sense

So, rather than trying to prove Noah's flood, arguing about the age of the Earth, what happened to the dinosours, or the inconsistencies of other religions, try explaining (gently and lovingly) how the law of God condemns unforgiveness as murder, and stealing and lying, even once, is a capital offense. Watch what happens when you tell a man that the seventh commandment condemns looking at women with lust or viewing pornography!

Have you ever had a dentist hit a nerve with a drill? I have seen many men break out in a cold sweat, others begin to shake, and still others literally break down in tears of repentance after seeing themselves in the mirror of God's law.

Sharing the Ten Commandments (defining sin) is *the* most compelling, convicting, embarrassing, politically incorrect, in-your-face, none-of-your-business, I cannot believe you are saying this to me, most personal, and most loving thing you can say to another human being. The power of Mt. Sinai has never diminished.

If you see someone driving the wrong way down a one way street, his life is potentially in danger. Isn't telling them they are going in the wrong direction the right thing to do?

> *Better are the wounds of a friend, than the kisses of an enemy (Prov. 27:6).*

> *Have I become your enemy because I tell you the truth? (Gal. 4:16).*

Here is how Noah Webster defined the word "moral" in *The 1828 American Dictionary of the English language,*

Moral 1. Relating to the practice, manners, or conduct of man as social beings in relation to each other, and with reference to right and wrong. The word moral is applicable to actions that are good or evil, virtual as or vicious, and has reference to the law of God as the standard by which their character is to be determined.

ONE ARGUMENT MORE COMPELLING THAN SOMEONE YOU KNOW COMING BACK FROM THE DEAD

In Luke 16:31, Jesus said that if the unsaved will not believe Moses, they would not believe even if someone came back from the dead to warn them of the judgment to come! How could they hear Moses? He had been dead for 1,500 years! Obviously, Jesus was referring to the moral law written on the human heart (Rom. 2:15).

In the *Matthew Henry Commentary* on that story, the great 19th century bible commentator said,

> Only a fool would think any method of conviction better than the one God has chosen and appointed.

As the late Dr. Walter Martin used to say,

> If they don't want Jesus, be sure and leave 'em with Moses.

In other words, if they don't want salvation as a free gift of grace, be sure to tell them exactly how good they will have to be to save themselves.

Since the Lord, in His mercy, has allowed me to understand how to "use the law lawfully" (1 Tim. 1:8), my "evangelical batting average" has gone through the roof! I have had the incredible privilege of leading many people to the Lord in tears of repentance.

> Those who are wise will shine as bright as the sky, and those who lead many to righteousness will shine like the stars forever (Dan. 12:3).

SMALL GROUP DISCUSSION QUESTIONS
FOR CHAPTER THREE

1. Why is there no excuse for unbelief, according to Romans 1:18-20?
2. Paraphrase this verse in your own words.
3. What is God saying in Psalm 19:1-3?
4. How does knowing this help you when it comes to sharing your faith?
5. Now look at Romans 2:15. What law is Paul referring to?
6. Why can't atheists find God?
7. What do we learn from John 7:17?
8. Read Luke 16:19-31. What do you think Jesus means by this?
9. What is the relationship between the law and Jesus Christ according to Galatians 3:24?
10. How does the Ceremonial Law (sacrificing animals) point us to Christ? How does the Moral Law (Ten Commandments) point us to Christ?

CHAPTER FOUR
GOD'S MASTER PLAN OF SALVATION

GOD'S MASTER PLAN OF SALVATION IS JESUS CHRIST!

For God so loved the world that He gave His only begotten Son, that whoever believes in Him should not perish but have everlasting life (John 3:16).

The origin of human life is the greatest mystery that has baffled thinking people for centuries. No credible person in all of recorded history has ever claimed to be the source of life itself - with one exception. Consider carefully the words of Christ!

Jesus said to him, "I am the way, the truth, and the life. No one comes to the Father except through Me" (John 14:6).

Jesus said to her, "I am the resurrection and the life. He who believes in Me, though he die, yet shall he live. And whoever lives and believes in Me shall never die. Do you believe this?" (John 11:25-26).

"Most assuredly, I say to you, he who believes in Me has everlasting life. I am the bread of life" (John 6:47-48).

And Jesus came and spoke to them, saying, "All authority has been given to Me in heaven and on earth" (Matt. 28:18).

And what does Jesus want to save us from? Sin and eternal separation from God! Those who reject Jesus, reject eternal life. Understanding the doctrine of sin is the key to understanding the infinite value of salvation and the price that was paid to secure it.

To the twenty-first century, post-Judeo-Christian mind (and for the vast majority of church members), sin is an abstract concept. It's not connected to anything. The problem with many would-be soul winners is that they offer the solution (God's grace) before the impenitent sinner sees the need.

To simply quote Rom. 3:23 and 6:23 to an unregenerate person, and expect them to be convicted by the word *sin*, is like getting arrested without being told what you are charged with! The average man on the street walks away from the typical "Gospel" presentation thinking to himself, "This guy is crazy. I'm not a sinner; I've never murdered anyone!"

In the back of his mind he compares himself to the people he hears about on the news and justifies himself. Willfully ignorant of God's standard of righteousness (sinless perfection), and deceived by the sin nature, he "suppresses the truth in unrighteousness" (Rom. 1:18), and lives in denial.

Since no one has defined sin for him (and being content not to search out the matter himself), he lives like he is never going to die. Sin (the key doctrine necessary to understanding the need for salvation), if mentioned at all, is just glossed over.

Most people think that since God is good, he will overlook a few minor transgressions. That would be like a criminal standing before a judge and saying, "Sure, I've committed a crime or two, but I didn't kill anyone, and after all, you're a good guy, can't you just overlook this one thing?" The judge would say, "You're right; I am a good person, and because I am good I must punish criminals.

Only a corrupt judge would allow a guilty person to escape the due penalty of the law. It is precisely because God is good (i.e., perfectly holy and just, that He must punish sin. To do otherwise would be to deny Himself.

J.C. RYLE

Ryle was a preacher's preacher in 19th century England. In his excellent book entitled *Holiness,* Ryle hit the nail on the head with his opening statement,

"The plain truth is that a right knowledge of sin lies at the root of all saving Christianity. Without it, such doctrines as justification, conversion, sanctification, are 'words and names' which convey no meaning to the mind.

"The first thing, therefore, that God does when He makes anyone a new creature in Christ, is to send light into his heart and show him that he is a guilty sinner. The material creation in Genesis began with 'light,' and so also does the spiritual creation.

"God shines into our hearts by the work of the Holy Spirit, and then spiritual life begins . . . I believe that one of the chief wants of the church . . . has been, and is, clearer, fuller teaching about sin."[1]

YOU CANNOT UNDERSTAND ANY OF THE THEOLOGICAL TERMS RELATED TO THE DOCTRINE OF SALVATION APART FROM THE DOCTRINE OF SIN.

Redemption: A term meaning "to release on payment of ransom." The idea is illustrated in buying a slave and setting him free. The question is, free from what? Eph. 1:7: "In whom we have *redemption* through his blood, the forgiveness of *sins*, according to the riches of his grace."

Salvation: A term meaning "to be saved, or to be delivered." The question is, saved or delivered from what? Matt. 1:21: "And she shall bring forth a son, and thou shalt call his name Jesus: for He shall *save* His people from their *sins*."

Justification: A legal term meaning "to be declared righteous." How and why do we need to be declared righteous? Rom. 5:8–9: "But God demonstrates His own love toward us, in that while we were yet *sinners*, Christ died for us. Much more then, having now been *justified* by His blood, we shall be saved from the wrath *of God* through Him."

Righteousness: An attribute of God Himself. 2 Cor. 5:21: "For he hath made him to be *sin* for us, who knew no *sin*; that we might be made the *righteousness* of God in him."

Sanctification: A term meaning "to be set apart." Set apart from what? Acts 26:18: "To open their eyes and turn them from darkness to light, and from the power of Satan to God, so that they may receive forgiveness of *sins* and a place among those who are *sanctified* by faith in me."

Gospel: Means "Good News." Mark 1:15: "The time is fulfilled, and the kingdom of God is at hand; repent [from sin] and believe in the Gospel."

The Cross: This was where the body of Christ was broken and His blood shed to satisfy the righteous demand of God's holy law against *sin*. "When Jesus therefore had received the sour wine, He said, 'It is finished!' (John 19:30)." The word "finished," literally means: "Paid in full." There is a direct correlation between God's love and the cross (see Jn. 3:16; Rom. 5:5, 6, 8; Eph. 2:4-5; 5:2, 25; 1 Jn. 3:16; 4:10 and Rev. 1:5).

There are two primary words used in the Bible to communicate the essence of sin. The first is *hamartia* (ham-ar-tee'-ah), translated in English as "sin." It literally means to "miss the mark and so not share in the prize." This word is well illustrated by a marksman shooting an arrow and missing the bull's eye. Romans 3:23 assures us that we have all "missed the mark."

The second word is *anomia* (an-om-ee'-ah), translated "transgression," which unlike "missing the mark" (because we were all born imperfect), refers to an act of willful disobedience. That is to willfully, knowingly violate God's law.

So, from these two words we learn that we are *all* sinners by nature, and we are *all* sinners by choice.

KEITH GREEN SAID IT WELL . . .

"Unless people are truly convicted of sin, if they don't fully see that they are totally condemned by the requirement of God's law, then it is virtually impossible to show them the need of a Savior. Why, what would they need to be saved from? fun? That is why our modern Gospel must dwell on 'all the good things God'll do for you if you'd just accept Him!'

"We can't convince a sinner that he needs a savior by just getting him to admit that, 'Well, generally, yes, I am a sinner.' He must see how the law of God totally condemns him as a sinner, and then the beauty of the Gospel, the glory of the cross, the marvelous power of Christ's blood will be able to penetrate his anxious, waiting mind and heart.

"But because there is so little real conviction of sin brought about by the preaching of our modern gospel, we cannot truly require repentance anymore. If we did, no one would 'come forward' at all.

"For repentance is easy to him who sees how ugly and horrible sin is, but repentance is impossible where the law does not convince the sinner of his wicked heart, compelling him to turn from his sin into the arms of a waiting, compassionate God.

"The natural tendency of the flesh is to avoid unpleasantness or discomfort, so we offer people a less confrontational, more indirect approach—something Jesus *never* did." [2]

Walking a person gently and lovingly through the Ten Commandments, and explaining the spiritual application of each one, showing how all of us have broken God's law in thought, word, and deed, is absolutely, positively, the most convicting (politically incorrect) thing you can say to another human being!

And, since Hell awaits those who refuse to believe, it is also the most loving thing you can do for someone.

Sadly, most people are unwilling to discuss these extremely personal issues. So, in order to avoid pain or embarrassment, we offer people a "Gospel" that has little or no conviction of sin. Just *believe* Jesus died for you, pray this prayer, and you're in! I have seen this over and over again by well-meaning, but misinformed people in the ministry.

PARADOXICALLY, ALL WE CAN DO TO GET INTO HEAVEN IS TO BELIEVE IN JESUS.

> *That if you confess with your mouth the Lord Jesus and believe in your heart that God has raised Him from the dead, you will be saved (Rom. 10:9).*

The question is, what does it mean to *believe*, and *what* am I supposed to believe? Even the demons "believe" in Jesus, and they fear Him, but you won't see them in heaven (Jas. 2:19).

The word *believe* is found in the Gospel of John ninety-six times, more than any other book of the Bible. The word translated "believe" in the English Bible comes from the Greek word *pisteuo* and is used as a verb; it's an action word!

It means: to believe in, to trust in, and to rely upon Christ alone for your salvation. It is derived from the same root word as the word *faith*. To *believe* in Jesus means to have *faith* in Jesus.

> *And without faith it is impossible to please Him for all who come to God must believe that He is, and that He is a rewarder of those who seek Him (Heb. 11:6).*

> *And after He had come into the house, the blind men came up to Him, and Jesus said to them, "Do you believe that I am able to do this?" They said to Him, "Yes, Lord." Then He touched their eyes, saying, "Be it done to you according to your faith" (Matt. 9:28-29).*

SO WHAT DOES IT MEAN TO HAVE FAITH?

As Ravi Zacharias reminds us, "In the Hebrew language, there is no word for faith, apart from the idea of faithfulness. In our being faithful to Him we find the purpose for which we were created. That is not bondage, that is liberating. Our faithfulness to Him is the key that unlocks the treasure of all that He has given to us."[3]

> *So then, men ought to regard us as servants of Christ and as those entrusted with the secret things of God. Now it is required that those who have been given a trust must prove faithful (1 Cor. 4:1-2).*
>
> *His master said to him, "Well done, good and faithful servant; you were faithful with a few things, I will put you in charge of many things, enter into the joy of your master" (Matt. 25:21).*

Genuine faith *in* Jesus results in a life of faithfulness *to* Jesus. Who were the epistles written to? "Paul, an apostle of Christ Jesus by the will of God, to the saints who are at Ephesus, and *who are* faithful in Christ Jesus" (Eph.1:1).

The question now becomes, what does it mean to be faithful?

> *He who believes in the Son has eternal life; but he who does not obey the Son shall not see life, but the wrath of God abides on him (John 3:36).*
>
> *When the Lord Jesus shall be revealed from heaven with His mighty angels in flaming fire, dealing out retribution to those who do not know God and to those who do not obey the Gospel of our Lord Jesus (2 Thes. 1:7–8).*
>
> *If you love Me, you will keep My commandments (John 14:15).*

Please note, when we talk about obeying God's commandments, we are talking about practical holiness from a heart of loving gratitude, *not salvation by our good works!* We do not obey Jesus to get saved. Loving obedience is the *result* of our salvation, never the cause of it (see Luke 18:13-14, Rom. 1:17, 3:20-24, 10:9, Gal. 3:24, Eph. 2:8-9, and Titus 2:11).

WHAT AM I SUPPOSED TO BELIEVE?

Who is Jesus? Is He a prophet, a priest, a king, a man, God incarnate, or all of the above? You can be wrong about a lot of things, but if you are wrong about who Jesus is, and what it means to believe in Him, you are wrong enough to spend eternity seperated from God. This is what He said in John 8:24,

> *I said therefore to you, that you shall die in your sins; for unless you believe that I am you shall die in your sins.*

There are seven "I am" sayings of Jesus in the New Testament. Each is a clear reference to Exodus 3:14 where God said to Moses, "I AM WHO I AM." And He said, "Thus you shall say to the children of Israel, 'I AM has sent me to you.'"

So, when Jesus said to the Pharisees, "Before Abraham was I am," they knew exactly what He meant, and wanted to stone Him for claiming to be God (Jn 8:58, 59 & 10:30,31).

Jesus said, "I am the light of the world," but, He did not just *say*, "I am the light of the world," He *said*, "I am the light of the world" and gave sight to a man born blind!

Jesus also said, "I am the bread of life," But, He did not just *say*, "I am the bread of life," He *said*, "I am the bread of life" and fed five thousand people with a few fish and a couple loaves of bread!

Jesus Christ said, "I am the resurrection and the life." But, He did not just *say*, "I am the resurrection and the life." He *said*, "I am the resurrection and the life" and called Lazarus back from the dead! Each of the "I am" sayings, were accompanied by a miracle which demonstrated attributes that belong to God alone.

The one miracle that Jesus performed more than any other was giving sight to the blind. Compare that to what God said in Exodus 4:11,

> *And the LORD said to him, "Who has made man's mouth? Or who makes him dumb or deaf, or seeing or blind? Is it not I, the LORD?*

These three "I am," sayings alone show Jesus to be the Creator, the Sustainer, and the Redeemer of mankind. How about when He said, "Peace be still," and the winds and the sea obeyed Him? And, what about, "Destroy this temple and in three days, I will raise it?" He was speaking of raising Himself from the dead! Only God can do that!

There are hundreds of examples of Christ's divinity in the New Testament, listing all of them is beyond the scope of this book. Here are just a few classic examples:

> For unto us a Child is born, Unto us a Son is given; And the government will be upon His shoulder. And His name will be called Wonderful, Counselor, Mighty God, Everlasting Father, Prince of Peace. Of the increase of His government and peace there will be no end. Upon the throne of David and over His kingdom, To order it and establish it with judgment and justice From that time forward, even forever (Isa. 9:6-7).

> And Jesus came and spoke to them, saying, "All authority has been given to Me in heaven and on earth. Go therefore and make disciples of all the nations, baptizing them in the name of the Father and of the Son and of the Holy Spirit, teaching them to observe all things that I have commanded you; and lo, I am with you always, even to the end of the age" (Matt. 28:18-20).

> In the beginning was the Word, and the Word was with God, and the Word was God. He was in the beginning with God (John 1:1-2). And the Word became flesh, and dwelt among us, and we beheld His glory, glory as of the only begotten from the Father, full of grace and truth. (John 1:14)

> I and the Father are one (John 10:30).

> Jesus said to him, "Have I been so long with you, and yet you have not come to know Me, Philip? He who has seen Me has seen the Father; how do you say, 'Show us the Father'" (John 14:9)?

> And not finding any way to bring him in because of the crowd, they went up on the roof and let him down through the tiles with his stretcher, right in the center, in front of Jesus. And seeing their faith, He said, "Friend, your sins are forgiven you." And the scribes and the Pharisees began to reason, saying, "Who is this who speaks blasphemies? Who can forgive sins, but God alone (Luke 5:19-21)?

> And after eight days again His disciples were inside, and Thomas with them. Jesus came, the doors having been shut, and stood in their midst, and said, "Peace be with you." Then He said to Thomas, "Reach here your finger, and see My hands; and reach here your hand, and put it into My side; and be not unbelieving, but believing." Thomas answered and said to Him, "My Lord and my God" (John 20:26-28).

Looking for the blessed hope and the appearing of the glory of our great God and Savior, Christ Jesus (Titus 2:13).

He is the image of the invisible God, the firstborn over all creation. For by Him all things were created that are in heaven and that are on Earth, visible and invisible, whether thrones or dominions or principalities or powers. All things were created through Him and for Him. And He is before all things, and in Him all things consist. And He is the head of the body, the church, who is the beginning, the firstborn from the dead, that in all things He may have the preeminence (Col. 1:15-18).

Jesus Christ, the same yesterday, today, and forever (Heb. 13:8).

I am the Alpha and the Omega, the Beginning and the End," says the Lord, "who is and who was and who is to come, the Almighty (Rev. 1:8)." I, Jesus, have sent My angel to testify to you these things in the churches. I am the Root and the Offspring of David, the Bright and Morning Star (Rev. 22:16).

SMALL GROUP DISCUSSION QUESTIONS FOR CHAPTER FOUR

1. Define redemption, salvation, justification, Gospel, and the cross. How does each relate to sin?
2. What is the difference between being a sinner by nature and a sinner by choice?
3. How do most people view themselves on the moral scale?
4. What can you do to help people see themselves as God sees them morally?
5. What does it mean to "believe" in Jesus?
6. What are we supposed to believe about Jesus?
7. What is the difference between intellectual assent and heart knowledge?
8. List some of the evidences that Jesus gave to prove He was God.
9. Name a Bible verse where Jesus claimed to be God.
10. How does Jesus claiming to be God affect all other religions?

Assignment for this chapter: Commit the Ten Commandments to memory.

CHAPTER FIVE
HOW TO PRESENT THE GOSPEL THE WAY JESUS DID

Ideally, I like to build a rapport with someone before I take them to Mt. Sinai, but that is not always possible. One day I was expecting a window salesman to come by and give me an estimate on two new windows for my home.

The phone rang, and it was Bob from the window company. He said he was just around the corner and wanted to come by a little early. I was in the study, and my children were eagerly looking out the living room window in anticipation of his arrival. A short time later I heard the children cry out, "He's here, He's here."

We all watched as the man got out of his car. Like any good salesman, he began to "read" our house. He was looking for clues that might reveal something about us.

Obviously, if a salesman can find a common denominator between himself and his client, he may be able to improve his chance of making the sale. Nothing wrong with that, just good salesmanship.

Well, our house is easy to read. There is a big cross in the living room window that lights up, and the bumper sticker on the car in the driveway said, "Study for Your Final Exam: Read the Bible!"

As I said, our house is easy to read. Now, I'm not making this up. This is exactly how it went, word for word.

I walked out to the side of the house and opened the gate. As my eyes met his, his first words were, "My dad was a Christian."

"Are you here from the window company?"

"And, my sister was a missionary!"

"You *are* from the window company!"

"Oh, yes. I'm from ABC Window Company, and I'm here to measure your windows."

He then proceeded to tell me all about his dad and his sister. I enjoy a good sales presentation, so I decided to hear him out. After about five minutes I asked, "Bob, can we look at the windows now?"

When he came back with his estimate, he went right back to talking about his dad and sister. After a couple minutes I asked, "Uh, excuse me, Bob, but, can I ask you a personal question?"

"Sure."

"You've been telling me a lot about your dad and your sister, but where do *you* stand with God?"

He said, "Oh, I'm fine."

At this point, I got excited, because I knew I had a golden opportunity standing right in front of me in my own yard. I said, "So, you believe in God?"

"Oh, yes."

"If you died tonight, would you go to heaven or hell?"

"I'd go to heaven . . ."

"On what basis?"

"Oh, I've been a good person."

"Do you see your need of God's forgiveness?"

"No. I've never murdered anyone!"

"I suppose if God compared you to Adolph Hitler, you'd probably compare very favorably. But, is that the standard God is going to use? Is He going to compare you to the worst person who ever lived and say, 'Compared to him you look pretty good. Come on in?'"

Bob shrugged and said, "I don't think so."

"Well, what standard is God going to use?"

"I don't know; I don't think anyone knows."

Now, I *really* got excited! I said, "Bob, I'm a chaplain at the Cook County Jail in Chicago, and there are ten thousand men locked up there, and they're all charged with a crime. If they're found guilty, they'll be judged according to the law.

"If you're driving down the road going twenty-five miles an hour over the limit, and you run into the man who wears the star, *you* too will be judged by the law!

"Do you want to know how you can know that the Ten Commandments were written by God and not by man? If man wrote 'em, there'd be ten commandments and a thousand amendments!

THE FIRST COMMANDMENT: YOU SHALL HAVE NO OTHER GODS BEFORE ME

"Stated positively, that means you *shall* 'Love the LORD your God with all your heart, mind, soul and strength.' That means from the day you were born until the day you die, you will never put anything before God.

"So, what does it mean to love God? Jesus said, 'If you love Me you will obey My commands.' But, God is perfect! Followed to its logical conclusion, to obey that commandment, according to God's standard, would require perfect obedience, which is another way of saying sinless perfection. No *mere* man has ever loved God like that!

"If the greatest commandment is to love God with all your heart, then the greatest sin cannot be murder. The greatest sin must be to not love the God who created you more than the things He created!"

THE SECOND COMMANDMENT: THOU SHALT NOT MAKE UNTO THEE ANY GRAVEN IMAGES

"You are not to make a god with your hands or with your mind. I have people tell me that my god is a god of love; he would never send anyone to hell. I agree with them. Their god would never send anyone to hell, because their god doesn't exist. He's a god made in their own image.

"The Bible says, 'God is a consuming fire,' He has a passion for justice, holiness, righteousness and truth, who will by no means clear the guilty, but will hold every man accountable for every idle word that he speaks.'"[1]

"You can be wrong about a lot of things, but if you are wrong about who Jesus is, and what it means to believe in Him, you are wrong enough to spend eternity seperated from God!

THE THIRD COMMANDMENT: YOU SHALL NOT TAKE THE NAME OF THE LORD IN VAIN

"When a man stubs his toe, he usually takes the name God or the name Jesus; the name that is above every other name, the name which represents a blessing, and uses it as a curse!

"The ancient Jew was so fearful of breaking this command he dared not even speak the most holy name of God, because the commandment goes on to say, 'the LORD will not leave him unpunished who takes His name in vain.'

THE FOURTH COMMANDMENT: REMEMBER THE SABBATH TO KEEP IT HOLY

"The idea here is to take one day out of seven, and to set aside all your worldly amusements, and any effort to better your position in this world, and just rest. And in that rest, acknowledge the God who created you, the God who sustains you, and the God who purchased your salvation with 'His own blood.'"

THE FIFTH COMMANDMENT: HONOR YOUR FATHER AND MOTHER

"In the Old Testament, to rebel against your parents was punishable by death. When you dishonor your father and mother you dishonor God, because He commanded us to honor our parents, and all in authority."

THE SIXTH COMMANDMENT: THOU SHALT NOT MURDER

"Jesus said, 'You have heard that it was said, "You shall not murder…" but I say to you that whoever is angry with his brother (or calls him empty headed or a fool) will be in danger of judgment and the fires of hell.'

"When someone does something wrong to you, and you 'decide' not to forgive that person, you have already crossed the line of sin. Jesus taught that we are to forgive even as we have been forgiven (Matt. 6:14,15).

"Second, when you choose not to forgive someone, you are putting yourself in the judgment seat of Christ; you are judging that person unworthy of forgiveness, which only God has the right to do. God says, 'Vengeance is mine; I will repay.'

"Third, refusing to forgive someone makes you a hypocrite with an arrogance beyond belief, because the very things you refuse to forgive in others (sin), you are guilty of yourself!

THE SEVENTH COMMANDMENT: THOU SHALT NOT COMMIT ADULTERY

"Jesus said, 'You have heard that it was said, "You shall not commit adultery." But I say to you that whoever looks at a woman to lust after her has committed adultery already, in his heart'.

THE EIGHTH COMMANDMENT: THOU SHALT NOT STEAL

"People are not thieves because they steal; they steal because they are thieves. Do you know how much you have to steal to be a thief? *Anything*! It's not the value of the thing, it's the principle of the thing.

"Jesus said, 'Whatever you do to the least of these my brethren you do to Me.' The Bible says, "thieves will not inherit the kingdom of God."

THE NINTH COMMANDMENT: THOU SHALT NOT LIE

"How many lies do you have to tell to be a liar? The same number of times Adam and Eve had to eat the forbidden fruit to be found in rebellion against God and worthy of death – just once.

"God says what He means and He means what He says. Revelation 21:8,

> All liars, their part will be in the lake of fire and brimstone which is the second death.

"If you're born once, you'll die twice. If you're born twice, you will die only once. The Bible says, 'It is appointed unto a man to die once, and then the judgment.'

THE TENTH COMMANDMENT IS: THOU SHALT NOT COVET

"Stated positively, it means: 'Be content with what you have'. That is, be content with what you can make with your own hands and your own mind. You are not supposed to desire what already belongs to your neighbor; including his house, his car, his wife, his title, his position, or his bank account."

At this point I asked, "Bob, do you see your need of God's forgiveness?"

He hung his head and said, "Yes!"

I went on to say . . .

THE GOSPEL

"In the Old Testament, an animal was offered as a sacrifice for sin. The animal had to be perfect, that is, without spot or blemish. Symbolic of moral purity, the spot was inherited, and the blemish was acquired.

"When the virgin Mary was impregnated, not by the seed of man but by the Spirit of God, what was begotten nine months later was God in a human body.

"Because Jesus was not born of the seed of Adam, He had no inherited sin (spot). And, because He kept the law I just described, He had no acquired sin (blemish). That is why the Bible refers to Him as 'The Lamb of God without spot or blemish.'

"When Jesus died on the cross, because He had no sin of His own, His death satisfied the righteous penalty of the law. God can legally declare sinners not only not guilty, but righteous, by virtue of the fact that an innocent substitute was provided on our behalf.

HOW DOES CHRIST'S DEATH APPLY TO YOU?

"While living in the Chicago area, I became engaged to the young lady who is now my wife, Susan. While it was the Lord's idea in the first place, I still wanted the blessing of my future in-laws who lived in Nevada.

"My fiancé flew out a few weeks before I did. When I arrived, they were expecting me. I knocked on the door, and without hesitation they invited me in. Later that night we had a wonderful dinner together.

"A few hours later, I was escorted to my own private bedroom, and told to, 'Make myself at home.' The next day, my future in-laws said, 'You're going to need to get around, so here's the key to the car!'

"Can you imagine what might have happened if I had knocked on the wrong door, a perfect stranger, and asked for food, a place to stay for the night, the keys to their car, and their daughter's hand in marriage? A sandwich may have been achievable, but the rest would have been out of the question!

"However, I was accepted and treated like their own son, because I knocked on the right door, I came in the right name, and I had the right motive—love! That is precisely how it works with God.

> *Therefore having been justified by faith, we have peace with God through our Lord Jesus Christ, through whom also we have obtained our introduction by faith into this grace in which we stand; and we exult in hope of the glory of God.*

"In the same way, when you come to God the Father in the name of His Son, Jesus, you are 'accepted in the beloved.' We are called 'children of God' and become 'co-heirs with Christ.'"

That is the Gospel in its literal, historical, and theological context, and the results speak for themselves. I cannot tell you how many people have broken down in tears after hearing God's law and God's grace presented in love, and how many others have said things like,

> I have been in church all my life, and never understood the Gospel until today. Thank you!

SMALL GROUP DISCUSSION QUESTIONS FOR CHAPTER SEVEN

1. How many of the Ten Commandments can you recite?
2. What are some key questions to ask before you share the Gospel?
3. If I could prove to you that Christianity was true would you become a Christian? If a person says "no" to that question, what is their real problem?
4. Give a simple illustration of grace.
5. How does Christ's death apply to you?
6. What do you know now about sharing the Gospel that you did not know before?
7. Why do you suppose it is that most Christians do not share the Gospel?
8. What does the Bible mean when it says, "To whom much is given, much is required?"
9. What do you think God may be trying to tell you in this chapter?
10. This week, share the Gospel with the at least two people. Then, share your experiences with one another. Pray for those you shared with before and after your encounter. Remember, only God can open a person's heart and mind to the Gospel. Your mission is to simply be obedient.

CHAPTER SIX

IS THIS REALLY NEW TESTAMENT THEOLOGY?

HEAR YE, HEAR YE, ALL RISE. THIS COURT IS NOW IN SESSION.

Opening statement for the Defense: Your Honor, ladies and gentlemen of the jury, I will now present my case by examining eyewitnesses from the New Testament.

These witnesses will provide irrefutable proof that Jesus, and the Apostles, used a method of evangelism that has been, for all practical purposes, entirely forsaken by modern evangelical methods.

In addition, we will provide you (the jury) with expert testimonies from a number of the world's foremost leading authorities in the art and science of Biblical interpretation. They will substantiate our claim, that there is one method of presenting the Gospel that is ordained by God, and as such, cannot be improved upon by man.

My final witness will be none other than our great God and Savior, the Lord Jesus Christ Himself!

FOR MY FIRST WITNESS, I CALL THE RICH YOUNG RULER TO THE STAND . . .

Defense: Rich, will you please tell the court your story?

The Rich Young Ruler: When I saw Jesus, I ran up to Him and fell on my knees before Him. I said, "Good teacher, what must I do to inherit eternal life?"

"Why do you call Me good? Jesus answered, "No one is good—except God alone. You know the commandments: Do not murder, do not commit adultery, do not steal, do not give false testimony, do not defraud, honor your father and mother.""

"Teacher," I declared, "all these I have kept since I was a youth."

Jesus looked at me and loved me. "One thing you lack," He said, "Go, sell everything you have and give to the poor, and you will have treasure in heaven. Then come, follow Me."

At this my face fell. I went away sad, because I had great wealth.

Defense: Your honor, ladies and gentleman of the jury, this was written for our instruction. A man comes to Jesus Christ and asks, "What must I do to be saved?"

The first thing Jesus did was to list 5 of the Ten Commandments.

Jesus replied, "You know the law. Thou shalt not murder, thou shalt not commit adultery, thou shalt not steal, thou shalt not lie, honor your father and your mother."

Jesus purposely omitted the tenth commandment which is, "Thou shalt not covet." The rich young ruler then says, "All these things I have done since I was a youth, what am I still lacking?"

Now comes the final blow. Jesus said, "Go sell everything you have and give it to the poor."

Rather than quoting the tenth commandment ("thou shalt not covet"), Jesus applied the text directly to the man's heart by asking a covetious person to do something a covetous person would not do! In order to reveal the true condition of the man's heart, Jesus Christ used the Ten Commandments as His standard!

Defense: Warren Wiersbe, To The Stand Please . . . .

Mr. Wiersbe, you are recognized the world over as an expert Bible commentator. How do you interpret this story?

Warren Wiersbe: "The rich ruler is a good example of the use of the law to reveal sin and show a man his need of a Savior . . . . [1] Why did Jesus bring up the commandments? Jesus did not introduce the law to show the young man how to be saved, but to show him that *he needed to be saved*. . . . [2] When Jesus quoted from the second table of the law, He did not quote the last commandment, 'Thou shalt not covet' (Ex. 20:17). Jesus knew the young man's heart . . . This young man was possessed by the love of money and he would not let go . . . . He wanted salvation on his terms, not God's, so he turned and went away in great sorrow."[3]

Defense: No further questions.

Judge: Would the State like to cross-examine?

State: Uh, not at this time, your Honor.

Judge: You may step down Rich. Next witness.

Defense: Your Honor, in 1910, A.C. Gaebelein produced a commentary that is still considered one of the most authoritative works ever produced on the book of Matthew. Mr. Gaebelein, do you have anything to add to what Mr. Wiersbe has testified to?

A.C. Gaebelein: I certainly do. Thank you. Your Honor, ladies and gentlemen of the jury . . . "The Lord . . . meets him on his own ground. The ground upon which he stands is the law, and with the law the Lord answers his question. How else could He treat him? The first need for him was to know himself a lost and helpless sinner. If the Lord had spoken of His grace, of eternal life as a free gift, he would not have understood Him at all. The law was needed to make known to him his desperate condition and to lay bare his heart."[4]

Defense: Thank you, Mr. Gaebelein. Your Honor, Jesus said to the rich young ruler, "Go, sell everything you have and give it to the poor." How would that have helped him?

Would he have been saved if he had gone out and given everything he had to the poor? Never! In spirit and in truth, this "command" to go and sell all he had and give it to the poor was given to reveal to him (and to us) the fact that his goods were his gods!

The Rich Young Ruler was in clear violation of the first (no other gods), the second (no idols), and the tenth (not to covet) commandments. The very law he thought he kept only revealed the true condition of his heart. "For where your treasure is, there your heart will be also" (Matt.6:21).

Defense: For my next witness, I call the woman at the well.

Madam, would you please tell the court your experience with Jesus on that fateful day?

Samaritan Woman: Well, as you know, I'm a Samaritan and a woman. I came to draw water from the well one day, and Jesus said to me, "Woman give me a drink." (His disciples had gone into the town to buy food.) I said to Him, "You are a Jew and I am a Samaritan woman. How can You ask me for a drink?" (For Jews do not associate with Samaritans.)

He replied: "If you knew the gift of God and who it is that asks you for a drink, you would have asked Me and I would have given you living water (John 4:10).

"Sir," I said, "You have nothing to draw with and the well is deep. Where can you get this living water? Are you greater than our father Jacob, who gave us the well and drank from it himself, as did also his sons and his flocks and herds" (vss. 11,12)?

Jesus answered: "Everyone who drinks this water will be thirsty again, but whoever drinks the water I give him will never thirst. Indeed, the water I give him will become in him a spring of water welling up to eternal life" (vss. 13,14).

At this point, I got excited. I said to Him, "Sir, give me this water so that I won't get thirsty and have to keep coming here to draw water" (vs. 15).

Jesus said to me, "Go, call your husband and come back" (vs. 16).

"I have no husband," I replied.

He then said, "You are right when you say you have no husband. The fact is, you have had five husbands, and the man you now have is not your husband (vss. 17,18).

"What you have just said is quite true, Sir," I replied. "I can see that You are a prophet . . . " (vs. 19). Then, leaving my water jar, I went back to the town and said to the people, "Come, see a man who told me everything I ever did. Could this be the Christ" (vss. 28,29)?

Defense: Your Honor, this woman asked Jesus for the living water, so she would never have to thirst again. The problem here is that she was talking about H2O, and He was talking about the Holy Spirit. Please note, the woman asked Jesus for a drink, and He did *not* give it to her!

The lesson is clear. The average "would-be" soul winner, upon hearing her request for a drink (completely oblivious to the fact that they were talking about two different things), would have immediately pulled out a tract and started offering her all the benefits of the Gospel before she understood why she needed it!

Jesus did *not* give her the "water," because she did not understand that ultimately her real need was not water, but the "washing with the water through the Word" (Eph. 5:26). Specifically, her real need was the conviction, confession, repentance, and forgiveness of sin!

Because the sin problem had not been dealt with yet, Jesus went right to the heart of the problem. When she said, "Give me a drink," He said, "Go call your husband!" On the surface, His answer seems irrelevant. What did calling her husband have to do with getting a drink? Everything! Look again . . .

Jesus said, "Go call your husband."

She said, "I have no husband."

Jesus replied, "You are correct, Madam. You have had five husbands, and the man you are *living with* now is *not* your husband!"

She brilliantly responded with, "Sir, I perceive that Thou art a prophet!" What was Jesus doing? Make no mistake about it. Just like the rich young ruler, Jesus was asking this woman to do something a licencious woman could not do. The Lord was referring her (and us) to the seventh commandment, which is "Thou shalt not commit adultery." Why? Because from Genesis to Revelation, God's Word assures us that those who do not repent from the practice of sexual immorality will not enter the kingdom of heaven!

> *Or do you not know that the unrighteous shall not inherit the kingdom of God? Do not be deceived; neither fornicators, nor idolaters, nor adulterers, nor effeminate, nor homosexuals, nor thieves, nor {the} covetous, nor drunkards, nor revilers, nor swindlers, shall inherit the kingdom of God (1 Cor. 6: 9–10).*

Judge: Would the State like to cross-examine?

State: Uh, no, your Honor. This doesn't exactly fit my theology, but I don't know how to refute it.

Judge: Very well. Call your next witness, Counselor.

Defense: I call Nicodemus to the stand (John 3:1-6). Nic, you were there. Tell us your story.

Nicodemus: Well, I'm a Pharisee and I'm a member of the Jewish ruling council. I came to Jesus at night and said, "Rabbi, we know you are a teacher who has come from God. For no one could perform the miraculous signs you are doing if God were not with him." In reply, Jesus declared,

> *Truly, truly, I say to you, unless one is born again, he cannot see the kingdom of God (vs. 3:3).*

Then I asked Him, "How can a man be born when he is old? He cannot enter a second time into his mother's womb and be born, can he?" Jesus said,

> *I tell you the truth, no one can enter the kingdom of God unless he is born of water and the Spirit. Flesh gives birth to flesh, but the Spirit gives birth to spirit.*

Defense: Thank you, Nic. You may step down. So, where do we see the law in this instance? The key word here, is the word *Pharisee*. The typical Pharisee thought his salvation was based on the fact that he was a descendent of Abraham. He believed he was on a one-way trip to heaven, based solely on his national and religious heritage (by keeping the *law* of Moses). His theology was totally backwards.

Nicodemus thought he was an in-law, when in fact he was an outlaw. According to Romans 3:20, the law that this Pharisee thought would save him was the very law that would condemn him! The Bible assures us that God does not have any grandchildren.

With that one statement, "You must be born again," Jesus was referring Nicodemus to his misunderstanding of the law. No one was *ever* saved by keeping it, because the perfect law demanded perfect obedience. "The law," as Leon Morris has pointed out,

> ...is the categorical imperative of God, by which men are accused and exposed as sinners.[6]

Human nature has not changed since the beginning of time, and will remain the same until the end. The people to whom Jesus witnessed were caught up in the same self-righteousness, self-justification, and love of the world as we are today. The names have changed, but the sin nature has not.

I would now like to call one of the greatest Bible commentators of the 20th century to the stand. I call Arthur W. Pink to the stand.

Arthur, what can you tell us about this most curious exchange between Jesus and Nicodemus?

A.W. Pink: Well, here is what I wrote in my commentary on John, word for word,

"What the sinner needs is to be 'born again,' and in order to do this he must have a Savior. And it is of these very things our Lord speaks to Nicodemus. Of what value is teaching to one who is 'dead in trespasses and sins,' and who is even now, under the condemnation of a holy God!

"A saved person is a fit subject for teaching, but what the unsaved need is preaching, preaching which will expose their depravity, exhibit their deep need of a Savior, and then and only then reveal the one who is mighty to save."[5]

Defense: Thank you, Mr. Pink.

Judge, here again we see the same pattern. Jesus asked Nicodemus to do something he could not do.

So, what do we learn from Jesus, the master evangelist?

THESE THREE PEOPLE REPRESENT THE VAST MAJORITY OF THE PEOPLE YOU WILL ENCOUNTER IN WITNESSING:

1. Nicodemus believed his salvation was in religion.
2. The woman at the well was blinded by her sin, and unaware of her true spiritual condition.
3. The rich young ruler thought he was a good person.

Jesus referred each of them directly or indirectly to the Ten Commandments!

THERE IS ONE EXCEPTION TO USING THE LAW . . .

If you meet a person under condemnation, who really believes his or her life has been so bad that God Himself cannot or will not forgive them, *this person does not need to be convicted by the law.* There is only one thing standing between this person and everlasting life, and that is a crystal-clear understanding of grace!

Remember the woman caught in the very act of adultery in Jn. 8:4? Jesus asked her, "Where are those who condemn you?" She said,

> There are none Lord.

Jesus replied,

> Neither do I condemn you. Go and sin no more.

Defense: Those who are broken and contrite, Jesus consoles with the Gospel, but to the proud and self-righteous He gave the law. For my final witness, I would like to ask Jesus Christ Himself to take the stand and settle this issue once and for all who have ears to hear. Lord?

Jesus: "Do not think that I came to destroy the Law or the Prophets. I did not come to destroy but to fulfill. For assuredly, I say to you, till heaven and earth pass away, one jot or one tittle will by no means pass from the law till all is fulfilled. Whoever therefore breaks one of the least of these commandments, and teaches men so, shall be called least in the kingdom of heaven; but whoever does and teaches them, he shall be called great in the kingdom of heaven" (Matt. 5:17-20).

Defense: Jesus, can you explain the story of Lazarus and the rich man in Luke 16:19-31?

"Now there was a certain rich man, and he habitually dressed in purple and fine linen, gaily living in splendor every day. And a certain poor man named Lazarus was laid at his gate, covered with sores, and longing to be fed with the *crumbs* which were falling from the rich man's table; besides, even the dogs were coming and licking his sores.

Now it came about that the poor man died and he was carried away by the angels to Abraham's bosom; and the rich man also died and was buried. And in Hades he lifted up his eyes, being in torment, and saw Abraham far away, and Lazarus in his bosom. And he cried out and said, "Father Abraham, have mercy on me, and send Lazarus, that he may dip the tip of his finger in water and cool off my tongue; for I am in agony in this flame."

But Abraham said, "Child, remember that during your life you received your good things, and likewise Lazarus bad things; but now he is being comforted here, and you are in agony." And besides all this, between us and you there is a great chasm fixed, in order that those who wish to come over from here to you may not be able, and *that* none may cross over from there to us."

And he said, "Then I beg you, Father, that you send him to my father's house—for I have five brothers—that he may warn them, lest they also come to this place of torment."

But Abraham said, "They have Moses and the Prophets; let them hear them." But he said, "No, Father Abraham, but if someone goes to them from the dead, they will repent!" But he said to him,

> *If they do not listen to Moses and the Prophets, neither will they be persuaded if someone rises from the dead.*

At this point, pandemonium broke out! Reporters ran to the phones to get the story out as quickly as possible. Jesus Himself had just said that using the law of Moses in the evangelistic encounter was a more compelling argument for Christianity than someone rising from the dead!

The lawyer for the A.C.L.U. just hung his head. And the judge banged his gavel, calling for order in the court! When order was finally restored, the judge asked if the state had anything at all.

State: I object, on the grounds of hyperdispensationalism. Nothing in the Bible is relevant to the Christian today prior to the book of Acts!

Defense: In Acts 3-4, just after the Holy Spirit filled the Apostles, Peters first two sermons bring about the greatest revival since Jonah preached to the Ninivites! His message was simple, "Turn or burn!"

In Acts 3, a lame man was healed and the people were greatly amazed. So, Peter preaches and in 3:14 tells them, "… you denied the Holy One… and *killed the Prince of life* whom God raised from the dead." (*Italics mine*). In 3:19 Petert said, "Repent therefore and be converted, that your sins may be blotted out." In 3:23 Peter, speaking of Jesus said, "And it shall be that every soul who will not hear that Prophet shall be utterly destroyed from among the people."

He accuses them of being murderers and sinners and will all be destroyed unless they repent, and 5,000 people got saved that day!

Then, in Acts 4:10-11, the Apostles were put in jail for the miracle performed and preaching Jesus. Here is what they said to the religious leaders,

> *let it be known to you all, and to all the people of Israel, that by the name of Jesus Christ of Nazareth,* whom you crucified, *whom God raised from the dead, by Him this man stands here before you whole* .

And, remember Acts 17 when Paul was in Athens? His spirit was provoked within him when he saw that the city was given over to idols. Paul stood in the midst of the Areopagus and said,

> *Men of Athens, I perceive that in all things you are very religious; for as I was passing through and considering the objects of your worship, I even found an altar with this inscription:*
>
> *TO THE UNKNOWN GOD.*
>
> *Therefore, the One whom you worship without knowing, Him I proclaim to you: God, who made the world and everything in it, since He is Lord of heaven and earth, does not dwell in temples made with hands. Nor is He worshiped with men's hands, as though He needed anything, since He gives to all life, breath, and all things.*

In order to bring the people out of idolatry and in to a correct concept of the one true living God, the foundation of Paul's arguments are the first two of the Ten Commandments.

In Galatians 3:24 Paul said,

> *The law is our schoolmaster to lead us to Christ that we might be justified (saved) by faith.*

That was *after* the Book of Acts! This hyperdispensationalist doctrine is heresy!

Judge: Overruled! Proceed.

I closed with this . . .

Defense: Your Honor, ladies and gentleman of the jury, as Luke wrote in his 16th chapter, things are crystal-clear. Jesus, in relating this story, is saying in no uncertain terms that you have a better chance of leading people to Christ by introducing them first to Moses than if their own grandmother came back from the dead to warn them of the judgment to come!

By God's grace, Matthew Henry, one of the most respected commentators of all time, understood this story perfectly. He said,

> Foolish men are apt to think any method of conviction better than that which God has chosen and appointed.[7]

The inevitable result of the knowledge of sin, is an overwhelming sense of gratitude for God's past, present, and future grace. This in turn produces a passion for loving obedience and a hatred for sin. At this point, we want to obey God not to get saved, but because salvation has already been provided; not in a law, but in a Person, and that Person is the Lord Jesus Christ!

FOR YOUR INFORMATION

You can be certain that the Ten Commandments were written by God and not by man, because:

- If man wrote them, there would be ten commandments and a thousand amendments.
- You can be sure they are divine, because every man from the beginning of time until the end of the world, whether or not they have ever read a Bible or even heard of Jesus, know in their heart it's wrong to murder, it's wrong to steal, it's wrong to lie, and it's wrong to have another man's wife!
- We know the Ten Commandments are divinely inspired, because between them and every other religion, philosophy, or system of thought, there is no possible term of comparison.

Think about it. Galatians 5:14 (a distillation of the Ten Commandments), says,

> For all the Law is fulfilled in one word, even in this: "You shall love your neighbor as yourself."

If we all cared about each other as much as we cared about ourselves, we would live in a perfect world!

Since time began, every one that has been born has died (with the exceptions of Enoch and Elijah, but that may still occur *if* they are the two witnesses of Rev. 11). Every death, establishes the fact that God's law is still in force. Every death proves that the Law is still in effect. The Law says, "If you sin, you shall surely die" (see Gen. 2:17; Rom. 6:23). I rest my case.

Judge: Does the State have anything at all?

State: Yes, Can someone tell me how to get saved!

Judge: This court is forced to the inescapable conclusion, based on Scripture and reason, that the New Testament is crystal clear on the place of the Ten Commandments in evangelism.

To begin with Moses and explain the New Testament application of each one of the Ten Commandments in the evangelistic encounter, is the most compelling and convicting method of preparing the heart for the Gospel. Furthermore, since this is the method Christ Himself used, and since nobody knows more about evangelism than Jesus, I hereby declare, by the authority of the Word of God, that, in the words of one evangelist,

> Evermore, the law must prepare the way for the Gospel. To overlook this in instructing souls is almost certain to result in false hope, the introduction of a false standard of Christian experience and to fill the church with false converts.

In closing, it is clear that God did not leave us to fend for ourselves in presenting His most precious truth. But rather, over the course of some 1,500 years, from Sinai to the cross, gave us a perfect picture of His own systematic theology of evangelism. As such, it cannot be improved upon by any man or man-made institution, no matter who they may be. My judgment is for the defense. Next case!

SMALL GROUP DISCUSSION QUESTIONS FOR CHAPTER FIVE

1. Romans 7:12-14 tells us the law is spiritual. Compare that to Matt. 5:21-22 and Matt. 5:27-28. What is the difference between the letter of the law and the spirit of the law?
2. According to this chapter, there are four basic categories unbelievers fall into. What are they, and what Biblical characters represents them?
3. What would you not say when sharing the Gospel with a person who is under condemnation? Why?
4. Why is the good news of Jesus dying on the cross for our sin so good?
5. What was the rich young ruler's problem?
6. What problem did the woman at the well have?
7. What problem did Nicodemus have?
8. What principle did Jesus use to show them their real need?
9. How do we know the Ten Commandments were written by God and not by man?
10. What did you learn from this chapter?

This chapter can be used as a drama to teach the principles of evangelism.

CHAPTER SEVEN
DON'T TAKE MY WORD FOR IT

I will never forget having dinner one night with a group of elders from a church, which included a man who held a prominent position with the largest evangelical association in the world. He was also a professor at a prominent seminary and had written a book on evangelism that sold over a million copies!

During our conversation, I was asked how my (this) book was coming along. I replied, "Very well, thank you." The professor inquired about the subject of my book, to which I replied, "Evangelism."

He immediately asked what the premise of my book was. I said, "The main ingredient missing from the modern approach to evangelism is the fact that the moral law prepares the heart for the Gospel."

One of the other men then asked the professor what his position on the matter was. Without hesitation he replied, *"Well, that is the classical position!"* In other words, that *is* the consensus of the greatest minds in the history of the church for the last 2,000 years!

And, he was right. That is the classical position. The greatest preachers in the history of the church understood how to use the law lawfully (1 Tim. 1:8) for the purpose of evangelism.

Yet, this clear New Testament truth has been, for all practical purposes, entirely forsaken by modern evangelical methods. This is the result of the dominance of liberalism in our seminaries which began sometime around the turn of the 20th century. I begin with Charles Haddon Spurgeon, who is considered one of the most brilliant men in the history of the church since the Apostles.

Charles Spurgeon: "Explain the Ten Commandments and obey the divine injunction: 'show my people their transgressions, and the house of Jacob their sins.' Open up the spirituality of the law as our Lord did, and show how it is broken by evil thoughts, intents, and imaginations. By this means many sinners will be pricked in their hearts."[1]

John Calvin: "We are certainly under the same obligation as they were; for there cannot be a doubt that the claim of absolute perfection which God made for His law is perpetually in force."[2]

John Wesley: When speaking of those who didn't use the law as a school-master, Wesley said, "All this proceeds from the deepest ignorance of the nature of the properties and use of the law. And, proves that those who act thus either know not Christ, are strangers to living faith, or are at least but babes in Christ, and as such are unskilled in the word of righteousness."[3]

Martin Luther: "The first duty of the Gospel preacher is to declare God's law and show the nature of sin. Why? Because it will act as a schoolmaster and bring him to everlasting life which is in Jesus Christ." [4]

D.L. Moody: "This is what God gives us the law for, to show us ourselves and our true colors."[5]

Matthew Henry: "There is no way of coming to that knowledge of sin which is necessary to repentance, but by comparing our hearts and lives by the law. Only a fool would think any method of conviction better than the one God has chosen and appointed."[6]

John Newton (who penned the words to "Amazing Grace"): "The correct understanding of the harmony between law and grace is to preserve oneself from being entangled by errors on the right hand and on the left."[7]

John Bunyan: "The man who does not know the nature of the Law cannot know the nature of sin. And he who does not know the nature of sin cannot know the nature of the Savior."[8]

Augustine: "Through the law, God opens man's eyes so that he sees his helplessness and by faith takes refuge to His mercy and is healed. The law was given in order that we might seek grace, grace was given in order that we might fulfill the law."[9]

Jonathan Edwards: "What good is it to have godly principles yet not know them? Why should God reveal His mind to us if we don't care enough to know what it is? Yet the only way we can know whether we are sinning is by knowing His moral law: 'By the law is the knowledge of sin'" (Rom. 3:20). [10]

Spurgeon: "I do not believe that any man can preach the gospel who does not preach the Law. The Law is the needle, and you cannot draw the silken thread of the gospel through a man's heart unless you first send the needle of the Law to make way for it. If men do not understand the Law, they will not feel they are sinners. And if they are not consciously sinners, they will never value the sin offering. There is no healing a man 'till the Law has wounded him, no making him alive 'till the Law has slain him."[11]

Wesley: "Therefore I cannot spare the Law one moment, no more than I can spare Christ, seeing I now want it as much to keep me to Christ, as I ever wanted it to bring me to Him. Otherwise this 'evil heart of unbelief' would immediately 'depart from the living God.' Indeed each is continually sending me to the other—the Law to Christ, and Christ to the Law."[12]

Martin Luther: "The law and the Gospel are given to the end that we may learn to know both how guilty we are, and to what again we should return."[13]

General William Booth: "The chief danger of the Twentieth Century will be religion without the Holy Ghost, Christianity without Christ, forgiveness without repentance, salvation without regeneration, politics without God . . . and heaven without hell." [14]

A.W. Pink: "The rest of the Scriptures are but a commentary on the Ten Commandments, either exciting us to obedience by arguments, alluring us by promises, or restraining us from transgressions by threatenings. Rightly understood, the precepts of the New Testament are but explications, amplifications and applications of the Ten Commandments."[15]

H.A. Ironside: "But that law so terrible to the sinner, is a law of liberty to the regenerated one, because it commands the very behavior in which the one born of God finds his joy and delight."[16]

Leon Morris: "The law of Moses is not a religion of salvation, it is the categorical imperative of God by which men are accused and exposed as sinners."[17]

Walter Kaiser: "The classic theme of all truly evangelical theology is the relationship of law and Gospel. In fact, so critical is a proper statement of this relationship ... that it can become one of the best ways to test both the greatness and the effectiveness of a truly biblical or evangelical theology."[18]

John MacArthur: "Evangelism must take the sinner and measure him against the perfect law of God so he can see his deficiency. A Gospel that deals only with human need, only with human feelings, only with human problems, lacks the true balance.

"That is why churches are full of people whose lives are essentially unchanged after their supposed conversion. "Most of these people, I am convinced, are unregenerate and grievously misled . . . We need to adjust our presentation of the Gospel.

"We cannot dismiss the fact that God hates sin and punishes sinners with eternal torment. How can we begin a gospel presentation by telling people on their way to hell that God has a wonderful plan for their lives? Scripture says, 'God is angry with the wicked every day'" (Ps. 7:11, KJV).[19]

Michael Horton: "Here indeed is a revelation of man's final sin, which Luther defined as the unwillingness to admit that he is a sinner."[20]

Kay Arthur: "The Old Covenant is the Law which came by Moses, and, believe it or not, it plays a vital role in bringing a man or woman to Christ. If we would use it more, we would probably not have so many *false* professions of salvation."[21]

Alexander Maclaren: Speaking on Romans 3:19-26, "Every word of God, whether promise, or doctrine, or specific command, has in it some element bearing on conduct. God reveals nothing only in order that we may know, but that, knowing, we may do and be what is pleasing in His sight. All His words are law.

"But Paul sets forth another view of its purpose here; namely, to drive home to men's consciences the conviction of sin. That is not the only purpose, for God reveals duty primarily in order that men may do it, and His law is meant to be obeyed.

"But, failing obedience, this second purpose comes into action, and His law is a swift witness against sin. The more clearly we know our duty, the more poignant will be our consciousness of failure.

"The light which shines which shows the path of right, shines to show our deviations from it. And that conviction of sin, which it was the very purpose of all the previous revelation to produce, is a merciful gift; for, as the Apostle implies, it is the prerequisite to the faith which saves." [22]

Donald Grey Barnhouse: Speaking on Romans 3:20, "Here we meet by far the most difficult Divine utterance for the human heart to yield to that we have met in the entire epistle. Even those without law—'Gentiles that have not the law' (of Moses—Rom. 2:14) we find throughout history so many committed to their ideas of what is 'right', that they will desperately fight for their convictions . . .

"It is much easier to detach a Chinese from the analects of Confucius and bring him to a knowledge of Christ, than it is to detach some people, born within the sphere of Christendom, from their hope of salvation by the golden rule. They are astonished when you tell them that Christ did not give them the golden rule as a formula for salvation, but as a means of revealing to man that he is fundamentally crooked (sinful, i.e., full of sin) and that therefore he needed a power outside himself.

"The law was a standard that was given in order to convince men of their own hopeless incapacity, so that they might come to God in grace. The law of God is like a mirror.

"Now the purpose is to reveal to you that your face is dirty, but the purpose of a mirror is not to wash your face. When you look in a mirror and find that your face is dirty, you do not then reach to take the mirror off the wall and attempt to rub it on your face as a cleansing agent.

"The purpose of the mirror is to drive you to the water. Any other use of the mirror is plain folly. It is by the straight edge of the law of God, whether expressed by Moses or reaffirmed by our Lord Himself, that man may know how crooked he really is, and may turn from the folly of self–effort to the reality of the life of faith in Christ.

"This new life furnishes us with power which we can never have of ourselves, and which will act within us. May God slay us with the law, in order that we might be raised from the dead by His gospel. For this is the true relationship between the two. Before God can ever give us the gospel, He must slay us with the law.

"The gospel is the power of resurrection; the law is the power of condemnation; and when the two are put together, they then serve their proper purpose."[23]

Jamieson, Fausset, Brown: Speaking on Romans 3:20, "How broad and how deep does the Apostle in this section lay the foundations of his great doctrine of justification by free grace—in the disorder of man's whole nature, the consequent universality of human guilt, the condemnation, by reason of the breach of divine law, of the whole world, and the impossibility of justification before God by obedience to that divine law!

"Only when these humiliating conclusions are accepted and felt, are we in a condition to appreciate and embrace the grace, next to be opened up. It is that which ascertains what sin is, shows how men have deviated from its righteous demands, and sentences them to death because they have broken it."[24]

Martyn Lloyd-Jones: "So that, finally, we can put it like this. The law was never given to save man, but it was given as a 'schoolmaster' to bring him to the Savior. The whole object and purpose of the law is to show that man can never save himself.

"Once he has understood the law and its spiritual meaning and content he knows that he cannot keep it. He is undone . . . It shows us our utter helplessness and hopelessness, and thereby it becomes 'our schoolmaster to lead us to Christ,' the only one who by the grace of God can save us, and deliver us, and reconcile us to God, and make us safe for all eternity."[25]

Alexander Mclaren: "The voice that spoke from Sinai reverberates in all lands . . . This voice like a trumpet on that day, waxes louder and louder as the years roll. Whose voice was it? The only answer explaining the supreme purity of the commandments, and their immortal freshness, is found in the first sentence of this paragraph, 'God spake all these words.'"[26]

Gleason Archer: "It was only the misunderstanding and misinterpretation of the law — as a system of merit-earning and self-justification — which is rejected in Romans 3 and Galatians 3 (and related passages). As for the Decalogue (Ex. 20:1–17), the whole basis of its sanctions is stated to be God's act of redemption by grace ('I am the Lord thy God, who brought thee out of . . . bondage')."[27]

R.C. Sproul: "He (Chemnintz) insists that the Christian church make a clear distinction between Law and gospel, but not a separation! If we see the Law of God as separated from the gospel of God, we would see these two ideas as being intrinsically and fundamentally opposed one to another.

"Now, if you confuse the two ideas: Law and gospel, then what happens is you either eliminate the Law by reducing it to a simple expression of the gospel, or you eliminate the gospel by making it a new Law. So, you have to distinguish between them. And what Cheminitz understood as the two great distortions of understanding Christian truth that have plagued the church not just from the first century, but from the Garden of Eden, have been the distortions of legalism and antinomianism.

"Legalism, in its simplest definition, is that error, indeed not just an error, but rank and deadly heresy that teaches that people can be saved through their own acts of righteousness, that people may be saved legally through performing the works of the Law.

"Antinomianism is the heresy that says, because we are not saved by the Law, but by the gospel, not by merit, but by grace, not by works, but by faith, that therefore the Christian life has nothing to do with law, nothing to do with obedience. That's antinomianism.

"And so, what Cheminitz and Luther were concerned about was this, that if you try to have the gospel in isolation from the Law, you are going to end somehow in antinomianism.

"If you try to have the Law without the gospel, you are going to end in legalism. Cheminitz makes the startling observation that the whole struggle of Israel in history, was the struggle over an understanding of the relationship between these two things, and he starts with Cain and Abel as exhibit 'A'; trying to answer the question, 'Why was it that Abel's sacrifice was accepted by God, and Cain's wasn't?'

"The answer that Cheminitz gives to that question is, 'because Abel made his offering by faith,' which meant, even in the making of the offering of worship and of praise before God, he came in a spirit of humility; understanding that the only way even this offering would be acceptable to God would be on the basis of divine grace and mercy.

"On the other hand, Cain was trusting in his performance. (The offering Cain brought represented the work of his own hands.) It's not by accident that the two greatest leaders of the sixteenth century reformation, both Luther and Calvin, were both deeply trained students in secular law before they embarked on a career in theology. They were students of jurisprudence, and they had a keen eye for the Old Testament law, and they saw what the Law was trying to show them; their own inadequacy."[28]

D. A. Carson: "If you begin (presenting the Gospel) with a massive view of God; of His holiness, of and the sheer ugliness and odiousness of sin, and of the terrors of judgment, then preaching justification brings immense relief! And with the relief, a sense of gratitude from which a great deal of Christian ethics springs. There is a tremendous amount of Christian ethic that springs from the sheer gratitude to the grace of God.

"If on the other hand you barely mention law, or God, or judgment, or terror, or hell, and then you preach justification, justification is very easily confused with a cheap grace decisionism. Then afterwards, you feel you have to whip people into shape with lots of talk about commitment.

"The fact that God spends two thousand years from Abraham to the cross, almost a millennium and a half from Sinai to the cross, to teach the function of law, to bring about a sense corporally in the people of God of the nature of transgression, and of the futility of human effort, and the critical importance of recognizing how lost we are.

"So, if then we now start evangelizing without presupposing any of that, or without people knowing any of that, we just dive right into a Jesus who meets your needs, however *you* define your needs, then it's not too surprising we start having distorted views on justification, and a lot of other things as well.

"If all we learn from chapter three of Galatians is the vastness of the fact that the law prepares the way for the Gospel, but do not grasp how and why it prepares the way, we will not apply it to people's lives appropriately. And then we will end up with a cheap Gospel, and then we will end up with such a diluted justification that there will be tremendous pressures to redefine justification, which is precisely what is going on now."[29]

Erwin W. Lutzer: "Christ's answer to legalism is that external obedience to the moral law must be coupled with a corresponding inner attitude of love and honesty. Christ's teaching was not intended to abrogate obedience to the moral law, but to add to its intended spirit." [30]

Erwin W. Lutzer: "I *always* start at Sinai *before* I take them to the cross!" [31]

Noah Webster's Dictionary: "Moral 1. Relating to the practice, manners or conduct of men as social beings in relation to each other, and with reference to right and wrong. The word moral is applicable to actions that are good or evil, virtuous or vicious, and has reference to the law of God as the standard by which their character is to be determined." [32]

SMALL GROUP DISCUSSION QUESTIONS
FOR CHAPTER SIX

1. Do you have a favorite quote. Why?
2. Read Matt. 22:36-40 and Gal. 5:14. The Bible itself says that its main message can be distilled into a single truth. What is that truth? Now read A. W. Pink's quote. What are the implications of Pink's statement?
3. How does the moral law apply to evangelism according to John MacArthur?
4. What is man's final sin according to Michael Horton and Martin Luther?
5. Many people mistakenly believe that you have to obey the Ten Commandments to get to heaven. How do Gleason Archer and Leon Morris help us understand that?
6. There are people who do not believe that the concept of law has anything to do with Christianity. What would you say to that person?
7. What are the proper uses and applications of God's moral law in our day and age?
8. What is the connection between the moral law and death?
9. What is legalism and what is antinomianism?
10. What did you learn from this chapter?

CHAPTER EIGHT

THE PERFECT LAW OF LIBERTY

When God says "No" to one thing, He is by implication saying "Yes" to something better! When the LORD said, "Thou shalt not lie," He was by implication saying, "You shall tell the truth." Lying is a sin, while knowing, living and loving the truth sets you free.

The Ten Commandments, like a coin, have two sides. On one side we see the law of condemnation and death (2 Cor. 3:7). On the other we see the perfect law of liberty (James 1:25 and 2:10). You are either a slave to sin, or you are a slave to righteousness, free to walk in the light of God's love, liberated from sin's power!

Christians are to walk in holy obedience, not to get saved, but because salvation has already been provided; not in a law, but in a person, and that person is the Lord Jesus Christ.

It was *after* God redeemed the Israelites that He gave them the Ten Commandments. That is why James 1:25 and 2:10 refer to them as the "perfect law of liberty." William Barclay, the great Scottish theologian, understood James perfectly,

> He calls it the Law of liberty; that is, the Law in the keeping of which a man finds his true liberty. All the great men have agreed that it is only in obeying the law of God that a man becomes truly free. So long as a man has to obey his own passions and emotions and desires, he is nothing less than a slave. It is when he accepts the will of God that he becomes really free.[1]

Allow me to take you on a tour of the Holy Land. I believe you will find this very helpful. We begin with a look at the preamble to the Ten Commandments.

Then God spoke all these words, saying, "I am the LORD your God, who brought you out of the land of Egypt, out of the house of slavery. You shall have no other gods before Me." (Exodus 20:1-3).

Consider the wealth of liberating knowledge found in this preamble to the law. First of all, consider the implications of the "I" in Exodus 20:2. This seemingly insignificant little *personal pronoun*, sets you free from the bondage of:

- Atheism: The idea that there is no God. So, how does an atheist account for the universe in which we live? Nobody + nothing = everything!
- Agnosticism: The idea that man is incapable of knowing if God exists. To know God is to have real purpose in your life!
- Polytheism: The Hindu doctrine of many gods. At last count they had 330 million gods. I don't know about you, but I have trouble remembering names as it is!
- Pantheism: The "New Age" (which is really not new at all) belief that God is all, and all is God.
- God being an obscure power or an impersonal force (i.e., the "Higher Power" of Alcoholics Anonymous).

THE NEXT STOP IN OUR TOUR OF THE HOLY LAND IS THE WORD "LORD"

God is inviting His people into a personal, love relationship! He introduces Himself to His people by revealing His most holy and proper name. I remind you that we see the grace of redemption before a word of law is uttered.

> *I am the LORD your God, who brought you out of the land of Egypt, out of the house of slavery.*

The word translated LORD in Hebrew, consists of four consonants, and no vowels. The English transliteration is YHWH (pronounced *yud-hey-vav-hey*). Theologians call it the Tetragrammaton.

To the ancient Jew, this name was so feared and revered they dared not even speak it, for fear of breaking the third commandment. This commandment states, "He who takes My name in vain will not go unpunished" (Ex. 20:7). As a result, the true pronunciation has been lost, but the meaning has not. It comes from the same root as the "I Am" of Exodus 3:14, pronounced, "I Ya."

That passage records the time when God appeared to Moses in the burning bush to give him his commission to deliver the Israelites from slavery. Moses, fearing even his own people would not believe him, asked God, "Who should I say sent me; what is Your name?" At that point God said to Moses,

> *I am who I am. Thus you shall say to the sons of Israel, I am has sent Me to you (Exodus 3:14).*

"I am" is a repetition of the verb "to be." It means the Eternal, Self-Existent One; the God who is, the God who was, and the God who always will be, from eternity past, to eternity future, without beginning and without end!

THE TEN COMMANDMENTS TEACH HOW TO LOVE GOD AND TO LOVE OUR NEIGHBOR

According to the New Testament, the Ten Commandments teach us how to love God with all of our hearts and how to love our neighbors as ourselves. This is the greatest thing you could ever know.

The moral law is divided into two "tables." The first four are vertical, and teach us how to love God. The next six are horizontal, and teach us how to love our fellow man. Rather than being mutually exclusive, law and love are mutually affinitive. Here is the law of love from Rom.13:8–10,

> *Owe nothing to anyone except to love one another; for he who loves his neighbor has fulfilled the Law. For this, "You shall not commit adultery, you shall not murder, you shall not steal, you shall not covet," and if there is any other commandment, it is summed up in this saying, "You shall love your neighbor as yourself." Love does no wrong to a neighbor; love therefore is the fulfillment of the Law"*

Thanks to the moral law, *love* can actually be weighed and measured against an objective standard. Without the guidelines of the law, love would be abstract and relative. In 1 Cor. 13, we see the attributes of love. The moral law defines its boundaries. In His infinite wisdom, God tells us that "love is the fulfillment of the law." If I truly love my neighbor, according to Romans 13, I will:

- Honor his marriage covenant, and mine, by not lusting after his wife.
- I will forgive him when he wrongs me, rather than committing murder.
- I will honor his property by not stealing it.
- I will tell him the truth (and what truth is) when I speak to him.
- I will rejoice in the blessings God has given him, rather than coveting his goods.

Here is how Jesus summarized the Ten Commandments:

> *Teacher, which is the greatest commandment in the Law? Jesus replied: "Love the Lord your God with all your heart and with all your soul and with all your mind. This is the first and greatest commandment. And the second is like it: Love your neighbor as yourself. All the Law and the Prophets hang on these two commandments" (Matthew 22:36–40).*

Jesus uses the words l*aw* and *love* in the same breath! He taught the same principle found in the first commandment in Matthew 6:33,

> *Seek first the kingdom of God and His righteousness and all these things shall be added unto you.*

Go back and read the context to discover what those things are.

THE FIRST LAW OF LIBERTY

When God said, "Thou shalt have no other gods before Me," He was saying: "You *shall* love the LORD your God with all your heart, soul, mind and strength" (Mk. 12:30).

This commandment speaks of God's right to exclusive allegiance since He is our Redeemer. So, what does this have to do with liberty? Everything! The first commandment answers the most profound questions any man can ask, namely:

- Who am I?
- Where did I come from?
- Why am I here?
- Where am I going?

This settles the identity crisis. If you are a believer, you are a child of God. When you know who you are in relation to, who He is, you find the purpose for which you were designed. That is not bondage, that is liberating. How does this set you free? For a man to be satisfied (free from insignificance), he needs three things:
- Something to do
- Someone to love (and be loved by)
- Something to hope for

How's this for a purpose statement?

> *But you are a chosen race, a royal priesthood, a holy nation, a people for God's own possession, that you may proclaim the excellencies of Him who has called you out of darkness into His marvelous light (1 Peter 2:9).*

According to 2 Cor. 5:20, you are an "ambassador for Christ." An ambassador is the highest-ranking official representing one nation (kingdom) to another. God has entrusted the church with the message of reconciliation. As representatives of God on Earth, our mission is to carry that message to a lost and dying world. This is a great privilege and an awesome responsibility. Is there a more noble cause?

THE SECOND LAW OF LIBERTY

"Thou shalt not make unto thee any graven images."

This is God's right to define Himself. The first commandment tells us who we are to worship and the second tells us how: "In spirit and in truth" (John 4:23,24). That is, by faith and according to God's Word.

This command warns against false worship. Over seven billion people now inhabit the Earth, and the vast majority of them "believe in God." Most of these "believers" identify themselves with one of the five major world religions:
- Christianity
- Islam
- Hinduism
- Buddhism
- Judaism.

Many people, unfamiliar with comparative religion, mistakenly believe that they are all basically the same, that all worship the same God, and as a result, believe there are "many ways to heaven." Nothing could be further from the truth.

The fact is, they are all mutually exclusive. They all claim to be divinely inspired, and all have vastly different definitions of the nature of God, and what He expects of us.

That being the case, there are only two logical conclusions: Either all of them are wrong, or one is right and the others are wrong! "If you step out into the middle of a busy street, it's either you, or the bus; it can't be both!" It is clear in 1 Tim. 2:5: "there is one God, *and* one mediator also between God and men, *the* man Christ Jesus."

CAN A PROPHET LIE?

One well known evangelist (who no longer wants to be associated with this story, for good reason shared this: He was entering a Muslim country and was asked to present his passport to the customs agent. The agent asked,

"For what purpose do you want to enter my country; what is your business?"

He answered, "I am a Christian evangelist. I have been invited by your country for a debate."

The man said, "Sir, I would like to ask you one question. What do you think of Mohammed?" The whole room became dead silent as all the other customs officials turned to hear his answer.

He said, "Sir, I would like to ask you a question."

The man said, "All right."

"Can a prophet lie?" The man thought for a moment, and answered,

"No, a prophet cannot lie."

"Mohammed was a prophet?"

Answer, "Yes."

Question, "Mohammed said Jesus was a prophet?"

Answer, "Yes."

"Jesus said He was God. If Jesus was right, Mohammed was wrong. And, if Jesus was wrong, Mohammed was still wrong because Mohammed said Jesus was right!"

The man stamped his passport and said, "Get out of here!"

SHOP, COMPARE, AND SAVE

- Buddha said, "I'm a teacher in search of truth,"
- Jesus said, "I am the truth."
- Confucius said, "I never claimed to be holy."
- Jesus said, "Which one of you convicts Me of sin?"
- Mohammed said, "Unless God covers me with a cloak of mercy I have no hope."
- Jesus said, "I am the resurrection and the life. He who believes in Me, though he die, yet shall he live."

None of these other men ever claimed to be God. They all said God is this way, go this way; and Jesus said . . .

- I am the way, the truth and the life, no man comes to the Father but by Me (John 14:6).

Idolatry is much more pervasive than most of us would care to admit. Simply stated, an idol is anything you love more than Jesus! And, since no mere man has ever loved God with all his heart, we are all guilty to one degree or another of idolatry.

Many if not most Christians have never studied the Bible; because they don't have time. We all have time for the things we really want to do. Research shows many people, spend most of their free time (the one life they have to live) watching the electronic idol. Idolatry is spiritual adultery (See James 4:4).

THE THIRD LAW OF LIBERTY

When God said, "Thou shalt not take the name of the Lord in vain," He was also saying, "Those who honor Me, I will honor" (1 Sam. 2:30). This commandment speaks of God's right to proper representation by His people and the blessing for those who do.

> *And whatever you do, do it heartily, as to the Lord and not to men, knowing that from the Lord you will receive the reward of the inheritance; for you serve the Lord Christ (Col. 3:23-25).*

THE FOURTH LAW OF LIBERTY

"Remember the Sabbath to keep it holy."

This reveals the fact that God has a right to our time, and the blessing for those who give it. Hebrews 4:9 says, "There remains therefore a Sabbath rest for the people of God." We can rest in the finished work of Christ on the cross. We are not to worry about the past (we can't change it), or the future (which is in God's hand).

This rest is intended to be a complete rest, physically, emotionally, and spiritually. Jesus is not just our Savior, He is our salvation. He is not just our Redeemer, He is our redemption.

There is nothing you can add to the cross of Christ. God purchased your salvation with His own blood (Acts 20:28) once and for all. Our good works are the result of our salvation, never the cause of it.

It is true, that while we live in this world we have great reason to be troubled, but thanks to Jesus Christ, we have even greater reason not to be. Our future is as bright as are the promises of God!

> *Let not your heart be troubled; you believe in God, believe also in Me. In My Father's house are many mansions; if it were not so, I would have told you. I go to prepare a place for you. And if I go and prepare a place for you, I will come again and receive you to Myself; that where I am, there you may be also (John 14:1–3).*

First John 5:13 says,

> *These things I have written to you who believe in the name of the Son of God, in order that you may know that you have eternal life.*

Now that is how I spell rest. Death has no sting, and the grave has no victory (1 Cor. 15:55). Real freedom is freedom from the guilt and the power of sin. Living in light of eternity is one of the most liberating truths you will ever learn. Here is a perfect example,

> *By faith Moses, when he had grown up, refused to be called the son of Pharaoh's daughter; choosing rather to endure ill-treatment with the people of God, than to enjoy the passing pleasures of sin; considering the reproach of Christ greater riches than the treasures of Egypt; for he was looking to the reward (Heb. 11:24–26).*

THE FIFTH LAW OF LIBERTY

"Honor thy father and thy mother."

This speaks of our parents right to respect and the blessing for those who do. It's the first commandment with promise: "that it may be well with you and you may live long on the earth" (Eph. 6:2-3). Why is honoring your father and your mother so important? God Himself is a picture of a family: Father, Son, and Holy Spirit. The foundational structure of every society is based on the family unit.

The reason our nation is in trouble is not because of crime, drugs, violence, divorce, etc. Those are only symptoms of the real problem. Our nation is in trouble because our churches are in trouble, and our churches are in trouble because our families are in trouble, and our families are in trouble because we have not trained our children to love God and love their neighbors as themselves.

Abraham Lincoln said, "The strenght of a nation lies in the homes of its people. As goes the family, so goes the nation." When you dishonor your parents, you effectively break the chain of command through which God's blessings were intended to flow.

How does this command liberate me? This is the first commandment with a promise, "That all may go well with you." The wellness extends to: personal, as a family, and as a nation. Jesus' final words in Matthew were,

Go and make disciples of all nations, baptizing them in the name of the Father, the Son and the Holy Spirit, teaching them to obey all that I have commanded you.

How do you disciple a nation? You start with one man, Abraham. Abraham had Isaac, Isaac had Jacob, Jacob had twelve sons who became the twelve tribes of the *nation* of Israel. They all *eventually* learned to honor God and their parents. That nation (one of the strongest on earth) is now more than 4,000 years old.

THE SIXTH LAW OF LIBERTY

When God said, "Thou shalt not murder," He was saying: "Forgive and you will be forgiven" (Matt. 6:14).

This speaks of our neighbors right to live and the blessing for those who love and forgive. Do you know what the number one psychological condition is of those who are admitted to mental institutions? Anger, and that anger is rooted in unforgiveness. When you refuse to forgive someone, you are the one in bondage. Unforgiveness is like drinking poison and hoping it will kill the person you won't forgive. When you choose to forgive someone, you are the one who gets *set free*.

One of the greatest Christians who ever lived was the Apostle Paul. Here is his secret to peace and happiness,

> *And so, as those who have been chosen of God, holy and beloved, put on a heart of compassion, kindness, humility, gentleness and patience; bearing with one another, and forgiving each other, whoever has a complaint against anyone; just as the Lord forgave you, so also should you. And beyond all these things put on love, which is the perfect bond of unity. And let the peace of Christ rule in your hearts, to which indeed you were called in one body; and be thankful (Col. 3:12–15).*

The cost of breaking this command? In the 20th century alone, between World War I, World War II, Korea, Vietnam, Hitler, Stalin, Mao, abortion, homicides, suicide, etc. It's estimated that 550 million people were murdered, which is more than in all the previous 6,000 years of recorded history combined! The 21st century began with a bang when 3,000 civilians were murdered on September 11, 2001 in New York City.

Statistically, we will not live to see the 22nd century. In light of the doscovery of the atomic bomb, Albert Einstein said, "The war that will be fought after the next one will be fought with sticks and stones" (See 2 Peter 3:10-13).

THE SEVENTH LAW OF LIBERTY

When God said, "Thou shalt not commit adultery," He was saying: "A man shall leave his father and his mother and cleave unto his wife."

This speaks of my neighbors right (and my right) to a secure marriage. Human sexuality is holy because it began in the mind of God. Faithfulness to one's martial partner in thought, word, and deed was God's plan from the beginning. The best research shows that husbands and wives who are faithful to each other have the most fulfilling marriages.

History tells us that in 165 B.C., a Greek king by the name of Antiochus Epiphanes sacrificed a pig on the holy altar before the temple in Jerusalem. This was referred to as an "abomination of desolation." That is something that is so unholy, so sacrilegious, it utterly desolates (spiritually) an object or place.

The Bible says "your body is the temple of the Holy Spirit" (1 Cor. 6:19). To take your body (the temple of God), and to join it in an unholy act, is analogous to the abomination of desolation.

In Psalm 51, King David pled with God not to take the Holy Spirit from him after he had committed adultery with Bathsheba. Sexual immorality of any kind is one sin that will bring bondage faster than any other. How does that enslave me? The lust of the flesh (like fire) is never satisfied (Prov. 27:20).

If you are not satisfied, you don't have peace and you're not free. Adultery is the highest act of treason a man can commit against God and his family. When Potiphar's wife was trying to seduce Joseph in the 39th chapter of Genesis, Joseph said,

> There is no one greater in this house than I, and he (Potiphar) has withheld nothing from me except you, because you are his wife. How then could I do this great evil, and sin against God (Gen. 39:9)?

The solution to the epidemic of immorality in our world, and its horrific consequences is simple. The law of liberty is found in 1 Cor. 7:2,

> Nevertheless, because of sexual immorality, let each man have his own wife, and let each woman have her own husband.

THE EIGHTH LAW OF LIBERTY

When God said, "Thou shalt not steal," He was saying, "It is more blessed to give than to receive" (Acts 20:35).

This speaks of my neighbors right to own personal property and the blessing of being generous. Any idea what the number one crime is in America? Retail theft. The cost? Billions. Who pays for it? We all do! The liberating principle behind this law is found in Ephesians 4:28,

> *Let a man work with his own hands that he might not have to steal any longer and that he might have to give to those who are in need.*

Let us remember that God commanded man to work before the Fall. Work is a good thing. God says,

> *If any man won't work, neither should he eat (2 Thess. 3:10).*

When Howard Hughes died, his estate was valued at over $1 billion. A reporter doing a story on Hughes, contacted one of the accountants who handled his estate, and asked, "How much did he leave?" The answer was, "All of it." Do you know how much of that money Hughes took with him when he died? None of it!

On the other end of the spectrum, there was a man of God by the name of George Mueller. George lived in nineteenth-century England, and dedicated his life to caring for orphans.

At the peak of his ministry, he was caring for ten thousand children! Imagine if you can, the job and the expense of providing housing, education, health care, clothing, and food for ten thousand children—every day, three times a day!

By today's standards, he raised millions of dollars, not for himself, but to provide for these children. It is reported that George Mueller died with less than $100 in the bank. Of all the money he raised, do you know how much he took with him? All of it, he sent it all ahead!

In the spiritual realm, whatever you keep you lose, but whatever you give away you keep. As the late Jim Elliot once said, "He is no fool who gives what he cannot keep, for that which he can never lose."

THE NINTH LAW OF LIBERTY

When God said, "Thou shalt not lie, He was by implication saying, "You shall know the truth and the truth shall make you free" (Jn. 8:32).

This speaks of our God given right to an honest hearing in court. Since lying is so commonplace in our world, it is inconceivable what would happen if everyone always told the truth. Much of our judicial system and our political system is based on lies. In many cases, it is the best liar who wins. But not for long. Here's a sobering truth from King Solomon, in Proverbs 21:6,

> *Getting treasures by a lying tongue*
> *Is the fleeting fantasy of those who seek death.*

There are many people who would never think of committing murder, adultery, or stealing, but think nothing of lying. After all, lying isn't such a big deal, is it? The first sin on Earth was when the serpent *lied* to Eve. That was the day when the covetousness of Adam and Eve embraced the lie of Satan, and the whole Earth was cursed as a result of one *little* lie!

Whenever I am tempted to sin, one of the most profound *truths* that comes to my rescue is the heart knowledge that sin always *lies*. It always promises pleasure, but it only produces pain! We will do well to remember that Satan is called "The father of lies," and Jesus said He is, "The way, the *truth* and the life" (Jn. 14:6).

By letting my "yes be yes" and my "no be no" (Jas. 5:12), I am reflecting the faithfulness of my heavenly Father. When I tell the truth, the Lord delights in me, which in turn fills me with joy. My conscience is clear, and I am free from the guilt and the power of falsehood and lies.

THE TENTH LAW OF LIBERTY

When God says, "Thou shalt not covet," He is also saying, "If we have food and clothes, with these we should be content" (1 Tim. 6:8).

This speaks of my neighbor's God given right to a secure life in the community. I remember seeing John Rockefeller on the news when I was just a child. He was being asked by reporters, "You're already a billionaire, Mr. Rockefeller; how much more do you need?" The answer was, "Just a little more son, just a little more." The principle of liberty found in this verse is learning to be content.

Lest you think covetousness is no big deal, it was Lucifer's lack of contentment that turned him into Satan. Col. 3:5-6 says,

> Therefore put to death your members which are on the earth: fornication, uncleanness, passion, evil desire, and covetousness, which is idolatry.

The Ten Commandments teach us *how* to love God and *how* to love our neighbors. This is the essence of "love" as revealed by God Himself in both the Old and New Testaments. Can you even begin to imagine what our world would be like if we all lived according to God's perfect law of liberty?

SMALL GROUP DISCUSSION QUESTIONS FOR CHAPTER EIGHT

1. How is it possible for the Ten Commandments to be the law of condemnation and death in one sense, and the perfect law of liberty in another? (see H.A. Ironside and William Barclay from Chapter Six for help).
2. What does the first commandment have to do with our true identity and purpose in life?
3. Read the blessings the curses in Deut. 28:1-64. What can we learn from this?
4. What does it mean to worship God in spirit and in truth?
5. When it comes to salvation, what is the one thing that separates Christianity from all other religions?
6. Share a time when you received or extended, or receieved grace to someone in your own life.
7. Read Hebrews 11:24-26. How does living in light of eternity help us now?
8. What should motivate us to share the Gospel?
9. What is the difference between the spirit and the letter of the law? (See Matt. 5:21, 22 and 5:27, 28).
10. How does sin enslave you? How is obedience liberating?

CHAPTER NINE

IF GOD IS GOOD, WHY IS THERE SO MUCH EVIL IN THE WORLD?

The number one objection people raise against God is based on the question of evil. If God is all powerful, why doesn't He remove all the evil people? It is a good thing He does not. If He removed all the evil people using His standard, none of us would still be here!

Nevertheless, the question of evil is a legitmate question that deserves an answer and the Bible provides it. The answer is only understood when we see it in the light of the cosmic struggle that has been raging for untold thousands of years between the forces of darkness and the Prince of Peace.

It began not in the Garden of Eden, but in Heaven. In Ezek. 28:12, God reveals the mystery of iniquity, and allows us to see exactly what happened before time began.

> *Thus says the Lord, "You had the seal of perfection, full of wisdom and perfect in beauty. You were in Eden, the garden of God; every precious stone adorned you: Your settings and mountings were made of gold; on the day you were created they were prepared.*
>
> *You were anointed as a guardian cherub, for so I ordained you. You were on the holy mount of God; you walked among the fiery stones.*
>
> *You were blameless in your ways from the day you were created, until unrighteousness was found in you.*
>
> *By the abundance of your trade you were internally filled with violence, and you sinned; therefore I have cast you as profane from the mountain of God.*

And I have destroyed you, O covering cherub, from the midst of the stones of fire. Your heart was lifted up because of your beauty; you corrupted your wisdom by reason of your splendor.

When God created the angels, He created one who was "full of wisdom and perfect in beauty." He was known as the "anointed cherub." I don't know about you, but I have never seen an angel. I do know, however, that they are *not* Caucasian females with long blonde hair, nor are they little babies with wings floating on clouds and playing harps!

According to the Bible, angels are extremely powerful creatures capable of performing feats of strength far beyond any mortal. In 2 Kings, chapter 19, we read the account of one angel that slew 185,000 men from the Assyrian army in one night!

If an angel suddenly appeared in your church next Sunday, no one would have their heads in the air, their faces would be in the dust! In the Garden of Gethsemane, Jesus said He could have called 12 legions of angels (Matt. 26:53), which would have been enough sword power to destroy the entire Roman army in less than a day.

The real battle, however, is "not against flesh and blood, but against the rulers, against the powers, against the world forces of this darkness, against the spiritual *forces* of wickedness in the heavenly places" (Eph. 6:12).

To get more on the story of what happened with Lucifer, we turn to the prophet Isaiah, written 750 years before Christ came to Earth. In Isa. 14:12-14 we read,

> *How you have fallen from heaven, O star of the morning, son of the dawn! You have been cut down to the Earth, you who have weakened the nations! But you said in your heart, "I will ascend to heaven; I will raise my throne above the stars of God, and I will sit on the mount of assembly in the recesses of the north. I will ascend above the heights of the clouds; I will make myself like the Most High."*

There you have it. The first sin in the universe—covetousness. Lucifer became discontented as the "guardian cherub, full of wisdom and perfect in beauty," he wanted to be worshipped! It was then that his name was changed from Lucifer (which means the light one) to Satan (which means the adversary).

THE REBELLION IN HEAVEN

It is believed (based on Rev. 12:4), that Lucifer convinced 1/3 of the angels to follow him instead of God. So, here we have 1/3 of the angels in opposition against God.

The question is, what should He do about it? Look at His options. He could have vaporized them instantaneously. He could have crushed the rebellion with a word! The problem with that approach would be obvious.

If the Creator had simply wiped out the fallen angels, the worship in Heaven would have been tainted by fear. We are assured in 1 Jn. 4:18-19 that . . .

> There is no fear in love; but perfect love casts out fear, because fear involves punishment, and the one who fears is not perfected in love. We love Him, because He first loved us.

Even though God is sovereign, one thing He cannot do is to make someone love Him. Forced love is a contradiction in terms. If God were to violate your free will here, true love would no longer be possible.

So, God said, in effect, I will prove my love, not with a show of force, but with a demonstration of perfect love. That is where we come in. We are exhibit "A" to all the host of Heaven that God is love.

> God so loved the world, that He gave His only begotten Son, that whoever believes in Him should not perish, but have eternal life (Jn. 3:16).

THE GARDEN OF EDEN

A close look at what happened in the Garden of Eden is most revealing. God created a small planet and set up a test for all to see. Man was placed in a perfect environment. Adam and Eve were created with a conscience, a free will, and without sin.

In Genesis 2, the Lord God gave them everything they needed to live in abundance. He provided Adam with a beautiful helpmate and told them, "Be fruitful and multiply." He said, "From any tree of the garden you may eat freely."

As He was about to leave them alone for their honeymoon (my paraphrased version), He turned around and said,

"Oh, by the way, there is one thing; just don't eat from the tree of the knowledge of good and evil, for in the day that you eat from it you shall surely die. Have a great day."

When the Lord forbid them to eat from the tree of the knowledge of good and evil, they were now put in the position where good was not the only thing they could do. The presentation of a choice to obey or disobey was now present, in order for man to be morally tested.

All the angels in Heaven were, and are watching God's plan of redemption unfold in real time. So, what happened? In Genesis 3,

> They both took from its fruit and ate; then the eyes of both of them were opened, and they knew that they were naked.

They chose to disobey God and as a result, the whole Earth was cursed with a curse. Question: Didn't God know that all this would happen beforehand? The answer is of course! That is why Rev. 13:8 says Jesus was, "the Lamb slain from before the foundation of the world."

GOD IS LOVE

God's greatest attributes (besides the fact that He is omnipotent, omniscient, and omnipresent), are His holiness and His love. His holiness, as seen in the moral law, demands perfect justice, while His love demands perfect mercy. That is exactly what the Ark of the Covenant represents. Inside are the Ten Commandments, which serve to remind us that we deserved death. But the law is covered by the Mercy Seat, which is sprinkled with the blood of Jesus Christ. The Ark of the Covenant serves as God's throne! He sits above the golden cherubim ruling and reigning in righteousness and truth, forever!

IF YOU ARE STILL UNSURE ABOUT ALL THIS, REMEMBER THE CONVERSATION BETWEEN GOD AND SATAN IN THE BOOK OF JOB.

"Now there was a day when the sons of God came to present themselves before the LORD, and Satan also came among them. And the LORD said to Satan, 'From where do you come?' Then Satan answered the LORD and said, 'From roaming about on the Earth and walking around on it.' And the LORD said to Satan, 'Have you considered My servant Job? For there is no one like him on the Earth, a blameless and upright man, fearing

God and turning away from evil.' Then Satan answered the LORD, 'Does Job fear God for nothing? Hast Thou not made a hedge about him and his house and all that he has, on every side? Thou hast blessed the work of his hands, and his possessions have increased in the land. But put forth Thy hand now and touch all that he has; he will surely curse Thee to Thy face.' Then the LORD said to Satan, 'Behold, all that he has is in your power, only do not put forth your hand on him.' So Satan departed from the presence of the LORD.

"Now it happened on the day when his sons and his daughters were in their oldest brother's house, that a messenger came to Job and said, 'The oxen were plowing and the donkeys feeding beside them,and the Sabeans attacked and took them. They also slew the servants with the edge of the sword, and I alone have escaped to tell you.' Another also came and said, 'The fire of God fell from heaven and burned up the sheep and the servants and consumed them, and I alone have escaped to tell you.' Another came and said, 'The Chaldeans made a raid, took the camels, slew the servants.' Another came and said, 'Your sons and your daughters were eating and drinking in their oldest brother's house,and a great wind came struck the house, and it fell on the young people and they died; and I alone have escaped to tell you.' Then Job arose and tore his robe and shaved his head, and he fell to the ground and worshipped.

And he said, 'Naked I came from my mother's womb, and naked I shall return there. The LORD gave and the LORD has taken away. Blessed be the name of the LORD.' Through all this Job did not sin nor did he blame God" (Job 1:6-2:10). But wait, there's more . . .

CHAPTER 2

"Again the LORD said to Satan, 'Have you considered My servant Job? For there is no one like him on the Earth, a blameless and upright man fearing God and turning away from evil. And he still holds fast his integrity, although you incited Me against him, to ruin him without cause.' And Satan answered the LORD and said, 'Skin for skin! Yes, all that a man has he will give for his life. However, put forth Thy hand, now, and touch his bone and his flesh; he will curse You to Your face.' So the LORD said to Satan, 'Behold, he is in your power, only spare his life.' Then Satan went out from the presence of the LORD, and smote Job with sore boils from head to foot! And he took a potsherd to scrape himself while he was sitting among the ashes. Then his wife said to him, 'Do you still hold fast your integrity? Curse God and die!' But he said to her, 'You speak as one of the foolish women speaks. Shall we indeed accept good from God and not accept adversity?' In all this Job did not sin with his lips" (Job 2:3-10).

LIFE IS A TEST

When it was all said and done, God restored unto Job twice as much as he had before! In this light, James 1:2-3 makes sense: "Consider it all joy, my brethren, when you encounter various trials, knowing that the testing of your faith produces endurance."

The staggering truth is that even the angels who have spent their entire existence in the presence of God are amazed at what a mortal man will do to please the God he has never seen! "In the same way, I tell you, there is joy in the presence of the angels of God over one sinner who repents" (Lk. 15:10). Can you imagine how God feels when His people praise Him in church, and pray to Him in the secret closet of prayer (i.e., when no one is looking)?

That is why Rev. 5:8 says, "And when He had taken the book, the four living creatures and the twenty-four elders fell down before the Lamb, having each one a harp, and golden bowls full of incense, which are the prayers of the saints." Obviously, our prayers are precious to God!

The church is God's chosen instrument to prove to the angels, the demons, and the world, that His love is perfect. Look at Eph. 3:8-11,

> To me, the very least of all saints, this grace was given, to preach to the Gentiles the unfathomable riches of Christ, and to bring to light what is the administration of the mystery which for ages has been hidden in God, who created all things; in order that the manifold wisdom of God might now be made known through the church to the rulers and the authorities in the heavenly places. This was in accordance with the eternal purpose which He carried out in Christ Jesus our Lord.

WHY IS GOD SILENT?

Imagine a young man driving up to an unmanned toll booth at three o'clock in the morning. The toll is 40 cents and all he has are two quarters. He is thinking about pulling away without paying just as he sees a police car pull up right behind him! Will he put in the money? Of course. The test comes when he thinks no one is looking. The quality of a man's spirituality is what he does or does not do when he thinks he is alone.

And there is no creature hidden from His sight, but all things are naked and open to the eyes of Him to whom we must give account (Heb. 4:13).

The New Testament teaches that there will be a war that will end all wars, the war of Armageddon. And, just before this planet is completely destroyed, God is going to stop it. In Matt. 24:22 Jesus said,

Unless those days were cut short, no flesh would be saved.

God is going to let sin run its course. He is going to allow man to rule his own destiny in order to show what happens when He is excluded from their plans.

So, when it is all said and done, there will never be another rebellion in Heaven again. No one will ever question God's integrity, His right to rule the universe, His motives, or His love again!

SMALL GROUP DISCUSSION QUESTIONS FOR CHAPTER NINE

1. Who is responsible for all the evil in this world?
2. What would happen if God removed all the evil people in our world? How many of us would be left?
3. Why can't God force someone to love him?
4. What purpose might the Ark of the Covenant serve in heaven? (See Rev. 11:19).
5. Why is God going to allow sin to run its course?
6. What does God want us to learn from Job?
7. The Christian has three enemies, the world, the flesh, and the devil. How does each one affect us negatively? Which one gives you the most trouble? Why, when, and how?
8. What is the significance of Rev. 5:8?
9. According to Eph. 3: 8-11, what is the function of the church?
10. What do you think God may be saying to you in this chapter?

CHAPTER TEN
THE FEAR OF MAN VS. THE FEAR OF GOD

When the Roman Empire ruled the world (with an iron first), it used all of its political and military power to try and stop Christianity from spreading. Meanwhile, the Apostles dedicated themselves to prayer and the ministry of the Word. Armed with the Gospel, and inflamed by the love of Christ, they turned the world upside down!

So, what made the first century church willing to be burned at the stake, boiled in oil, fed to the lions, and be crucified rather than deny Christ? Understanding the whole counsel of God is the key!

Sharing the Gospel, now that you know how, is no longer a question of fear, but of love. The real question is, "Do I love God enough to obey Him, and do I love my neighbor enough to tell him the truth?"

A.W. Tozer once said,

> We who preach the Gospel must not think of ourselves as public relations agents sent to establish good will between Christ and the world. We are not diplomats but prophets, and our message is not a compromise but an ultimatum!

Proverbs 29:25 says, "The fear of man is a snare, but he who trusts in the Lord will be set on high." The word translated "snare" is a word picture of a hunter setting a trap. 1 Peter 5:8 says,

> *Be of sober spirit, be on the alert. Your adversary, the devil, prowls about like a roaring lion, seeking someone to devour.*

The hunter is Satan and you, Christian, are the hunted one. Satan spreads the net, and the fear of man drives people into it. Sometimes it's blatant, sometimes it's subtle. We smile when we should frown; we laugh when we should remain silent; or worse, we remain silent when we should speak.

A MIND IS A TERRIBLE THING TO WASTE

I hear of Christian college students in secular universities who are so intimidated by their atheistic professors that they dare not speak up for their faith for fear of being ridiculed publicly.

I read of one college professor who says to his freshman class, every year on the first day, "Has anyone ever seen God?" (Imagine the intimidation that must exist in this type of atmosphere.) He follows with, "Has anyone ever heard God? Has anyone ever touched God? He follows with a warning that if anyone in his class has faith in any so-called deity, by the time he's done with the first semester, he will have successfully shredded their faith.

Some of these "Nutty Professors" have so many degrees, they don't have any temperature left! I would like to ask the class a few questions. I'd like to ask, "Has anyone seen the professor's brain? Has anyone ever heard the professor's brain? Has anyone ever touched the professor's brain? Well, based on the professor's own logic, we are forced to the inescapable conclusion that our professor is brainless!"

PREACHING IS WEAK IN MANY CHURCHES

Generally speaking, in America church discipline is virtually nonexistent. The reason? Pastors and elders are afraid of offending people. The thinking is, if we offend people they might leave and go to another church. Preaching is weak in many churches for the same reason. So is the worship.

Sometimes when I am in church on Sunday I become so overwhelmed when the worship is being offered up, and I think of where the Lord has taken me from, sometimes I just close my eyes and lift my hands. This position is the universal gesture of surrender, and also the universal gesture of victory.

There are people who mistakenly associate this with a particular sect of Christianity. I associate it with Paul's letter to his young protégé Timothy where he said, "I want men everywhere to lift up holy hands unto the Lord" (1 Tim. 2:8).

After church one day, a lady came up to me and said, "I wish I had the courage to raise my hands in church." This lady was afraid of being perceived as a religious fanatic in her own church!

In John 5:44, Jesus said,

> *How can you believe, when you receive glory from one another, and you do not seek the glory that is from the one and only God?*

Jesus is saying how can you possibly be a Christian if you live for the praise of men but you are not seeking to honor God?

I believe one of the main reasons people reject the Gospel of Jesus Christ is not that they can't believe, it's that they won't. Many people know that if they become a Christian, that would require a radical change in their lifestyle. And, how would they be perceived by their friends and neighbors? What a terrible reason to go to hell. One of the worst things about being in hell will be the knowledge that you didn't have to go there. I don't believe in peer pressure, I believe in pressuring my peers. In John 7:17 Jesus said,

> *If any man is willing to do my will, he will know of my teaching, whether I speak of Myself or whether I speak for God.*

THE BIBLE HAS A LOT TO SAY ABOUT THE FEAR OF MAN.

The father of our faith, Abraham, was willing to give up his wife to another man, not once but twice, because he feared what man might do to him. His son, Isaac, did the same thing with his wife, Rebecca.

The first king of Israel, Saul, was one of the most pathetic cases in all the Bible. The Word says he offered a sacrifice he was not qualified to make because he feared the people. God rejected him as a result.

MAY I BE EXCUSED, PLEASE?

In the Old Testament, you were excused from war for any one of three reasons: (1) if you had just married a wife, (2) if you had planted a vineyard and had not tasted the fruit of the vine, or (3) if you were afraid. Why would being afraid excuse you? Because the morale of one man had the potential of destroying the morale of the entire army.

When God called Gideon to go to battle against the Midianites, He said (in effect), "Gideon, I want you to go to battle, and I'm going to guarantee you the victory. The problem is, you have too many men. Tell everybody who's afraid they can go home." He had 32,000 men, and 22,000 of them jumped up and said, "Thank you, Jesus!" (my paraphrase) and went home!

Gideon needed to get his army down to 300 men before God would be assured of getting the glory for the victory. The points to this story are:

- The battles and their outcomes belong to the Lord.
- God can do more with 300 people who are totally sold-out to Jesus than He can with 32,000 part-time, half-hearted, pew warmers, and layabouts.

WHAT DOES A THREE-THOUSAND-YEAR-OLD, UNCIRCUMCISED PHILISTINE HAVE TO DO WITH ME?

Remember the story of David and Goliath? The Philistines on one side represent the world. They send out their champion, the best the world has to offer, and they challenge the people of God to do battle. What's at stake? God's name, God's word, and God's reputation!

Saul, the King of Israel, and the Israelites all "believed" in God. Well, "even the demons believe in God" (James 2:19).

David came on the scene, heard the giant's threats, and understood that the battle belonged to the Lord. The difference bewteen the Israelites and David was profound. The Israelites believed *in* God, but David *believed* God! Almost everybody believes in God, precious few actually believe Him.

THE CLASSIC EXAMPLE

The classic example of the fear of man surely must be the history of the Israelites failing to take the Promised Land in Numbers chapter 13. God had promised the Israelites a piece of real estate through which they would establish a nation charged with bringing the message of redemption and the Redeemer in to the world.

It was called the Promised Land because God promised it to them. Furthermore, it was referred to as, "The land that flowed with milk and honey," a picture of abundance.

They sent in 12 leaders to spy out the land. So, 12 spies go in and 12 spies come out. Two of them, Joshua and Caleb said, "Let's roll. God is with us." The remaining 10 said, "The walls are well fortified, we saw giants in the land, and we were grasshoppers in our own sight." The 10 we thought were warriors were actually wimps.

These were the same people who witnessed the power of God with their own eyes at Mt. Sinai., yet when it came time to obey God, they feared man more than God. The LORD called their lack of faith, rebellion; and His judgment was recorded for us. That faithless generation never got the blessing. Only Joshua and Caleb and those 20 years old and younger were allowed to enter the land of promise—40 years later!

WHAT DOES ALL THIS HAVE TO DO WITH YOU? EVERYTHING!

First Corinthians chapter 10 and Romans 15:4 tell us, the things that happened to the Israelites in the Old Testament were written for our instruction and for our example. God didn't want the church to make the same mistake, and unfortunately, we are. Here's how I know that.

Statistically, 95% of people who claim to be "Christians" have never even attempted to lead another person to Christ, and 71% of them think it is wrong to interfere with another person's belief-system!

In light of the fact that the Great Commission to the church is to, "Go and make disciples of all nations," and since most Christians have never even attempted to lead another person to Christ, it's the same rebellion. Will they enter the Promised Land or remain in the wilderness?

Three times in Matthew chapter 10 Jesus said, "Do not fear man."

> *And do not fear those who kill the body, but are unable to kill the soul; but rather fear Him who is able to destroy both soul and body in hell.*

THE GUN THAT KILLS WITHOUT BULLETS

The fear of man is just like a gun without bullets. You can scare a lot of people with a gun, even if it has no bullets. However, its power is purely psychological. It has no real power. The fear of man is just like that. It's not there. It's all in the mind!

If someone puts a gun to my head and says, "Renounce Christ, or I'll take your life," I would have to say, "You mean you're threatening me with heaven? Go ahead, make my day!"

For the Christian, death is not the end; it's the glorious beginning. You haven't found anything worth living for until you've found something worth dying for.

DINNER FOR TWO?

Picture this: You go out to a great restaurant with your spouse. The hostess asks, "Table for two?"

Your spouse replies, "We would like separate tables, please."

You ask, "Why would we do that?"

She says, "Well, I wouldn't want anybody to see us together."

You reply, "Why not?"

She whispers, "Well, I wouldn't want anyone to know we are married."

How would you feel? How do you think it makes God feel when we are embarrassed or ashamed to be seen with Him in public?

How do you think it makes Jesus feel when a homosexual "comes out of the closet" and declares to the world his or her sexual perversion, while many Christians are terrified to even mention the name of Jesus in public? It's time for Christians to come out of the closet, unless you're praying.

JESUS CHRIST

Therefore whoever confesses Me before men, him I will also confess before My Father who is in heaven. But whoever denies Me before men, him I will also deny before My Father who is in heaven (Matt. 10:32).

The first time I read this verse, I was so convicted. I knew that if I was really a Christian, I would have to tell all my friends about Jesus. The problem was, I was afraid of being labeled a "Jesus Freak" or a "Religious Fanatic."

God was saying that if you are really a Christian, there is no such thing as neutral ground. You're either part of the problem, or part of the solution. You're either an asset, or a liability. In His own words, "You either gather with Me or you scatter" (Matt. 12:30).

So, I prayed and said, "Lord, if you'll take that fear of man away from me, I'll never miss an opportunity to speak for You. Wherever I am, whatever I'm doing, if I feel Your elbow in my ribs, I'll say whatever you want me to say to whomever you want me to say it." At the time, I had no idea that 1 John 5:14 said,

> Now this is the confidence that we have in Him, that if we ask anything according to His will, He hears us. And if we know that He hears us, whatever we ask, we know that we have the petitions that we have asked of Him.

I "believed" in Jesus when I was fifteen years old. I "believed" so strongly, I "believed" I would have died for Him rather than renounce my faith. My problem was, I wasn't living for Him. I realize now that ours is not the "god of the dead; He's the God of the living" (Mk. 12:27). He didn't want me to die for Him (necessarily); He wanted me to live for Him. He's not looking for dead sacrifices anymore.

By God's grace, "I am no longer ashamed of the Gospel, for I know it is the power of God unto salvation to all who believe" (Rom. 1:16). Some people do think I'm a "Jesus Freak," and some do think I'm a "Religious Fanatic," but God calls me son!

THE FEAR OF MAN IS IDOLATRY.

Idolatry is rival worship. In Isaiah 57:11, God asks,

> Whom have you so dreaded and feared that you have been false to Me, and have neither remembered me, nor pondered this in your hearts? Is it not because I have long been silent that you do not fear Me?

The implication is clear, to be more concerned about what men think than what God thinks is to be false to Him! Let me ask you, when you die, will you bow before them in worship? Listen to what God says in Isaiah 51:12,

> I, even I, am He who comforts you. Who are you that you are afraid of man who will die, and of the son of man who is made like grass?

I don't mean to brag, but I'm not afraid of grass at all. In fact, I cut the grass at home. In all honesty, I would not be afraid if there was a whole bail of hay behind me right now ready to jump me!

God is saying, "Let's look at it in perspective. A man may live for seventy or eighty years, then he dies, only to stand before Me. I am the God who is, the God who was, and the God who always will be. Why are you afraid of a man who is like grass? A man can't save you, and a man can't condemn you."

HOW DO WE GET DELIVERED?

I think I've defined the problem. Now, let's talk about the solution. How do we get delivered? Deliverance from any sin is a work of grace. A work of grace is something only God can do. Paradoxically, our part must be factored in! Gal. 5:22-23 says,

> . . . the fruit of the Spirit is self-control.

Our part has three basic components:

#1 Prayer Appeal to the grace of God. Pray and ask Him to deliver you from the fear of man.

> Now this is the confidence that we have in Him, that if we ask anything according to His will, He hears us. And if we know that He hears us, whatever we ask, we know that we have the petitions that we have asked of Him (1 John 5:14-15).

#2 Study The Word Of God

The better you know the Word of God the better you know the God of the Word. The answer to our immediate problem is right in the text. "The fear of man is a snare but he who trusts in the LORD will be set on high."

The key word here is LORD = YHWH, in Hebrew. This is God's most holy and proper name. It means "The Eternal, self-existent One." The

God who is, was, and always will be, from eternity past to eternity future, without beginning and without end.

God wants us to live in light of eternity.

> *For what will a man be profited, if he gains the whole world, and forfeits his soul? Or what will a man give in exchange for his soul (Matt. 16:26)?*

> *By faith, Moses, when he became of age, refused to be called the son of Pharaoh's daughter, choosing rather to suffer affliction with the people of God than to enjoy the passing pleasures of sin, esteeming the reproach of Christ greater riches than the treasures in Egypt; for he looked to the reward (Heb. 11:24).*

Sadly, many never study the Word of God from cover to cover. You don't have to be a rocket scientist to figure out that if you spend nine years in front of the TV, compared to four months in church, and never seriously study the Word of God, spiritually/intellectually, you will remain a babe in Christ, unskilled in the Word of righteousness. You will never know the abundant life Jesus intended for His followers. So, let's take your temperature:

- Is Jesus Christ, His work, His church, His kingdom, your number one passion in life?
- Is Jesus Christ your favorite thing to talk about and spend your money on?
- If you didn't know any more about your business or profession than you do about the Bible after the same number of years of exposure, where would you be in your business or profession today? Would you be bankrupt or fired?
- If it were against the law to be a Christian, and you were charged with being a Christian, would there be enough evidence to convict you in a court of law? Would your neighbors testify against you?
- Does anyone know you are a Christian, or are you the only one? Because, if you are the only person who knows it, there is a good chance you may not be one.
- Do you have a passion for lost souls? If you do not have a passion to see people get saved, are you sure you're saved?

#3 Know Why You Believe What You Believe

1 Peter 3:15-16 tells us, "But sanctify the Lord God in your hearts, and always be ready to give a defense to everyone who asks you a reason for the hope that is in you, with meekness and fear."

Learn how to present the Gospel, then go out and do it. That is the whole point of this book. Find someone who is involved in front-line ministry. Go with them on a regular basis. It gets easier all the time. Go to: a jail, a homeless shelter, a nursing home, or in front of a criminal court building. Offer to pray with people, hand out tracts there, and almost everyone will accept them. It's spiritually exhilarating. Here's a prime example.

PHIL MEETS A NAZI

It was a beautiful Saturday afternoon in the city of Chicago. As a chaplain, I had to go down to the Cook County Jail to take care of some administrative duties with my volunteers. When we finished, we decided to stop at a Mexican restaurant for lunch. We were laughing and having a good time enjoying the presence of the Lord. Just then four men walked in with a very dark countenance. They sat right behind us.

They were speaking louder than we were, and in a very foreign language. My wife, who is as bold as a lion, turned around and asked, "Excuse me, but are you speaking Farsi?" Surprisingly, they answered "Yes. How did you know?" My wife said, "I come from an Armenian and an Assyrian background, and I recognize Farsi when I hear it."

Usually when an Armenian or an Assyrian meets one of their own, it's as if Middle Eastern music comes out of the sky, they pull out the handkerchiefs, and start dancing around the room! These guys however were not interested in dancing with us. So, they all turned around and returned to their conversations.

My wife turned to me, leaned forward, and whispered, "They're Muslims"! I said, "Nah," she said, "Oh yes, they are!" So, I said to them, "Excuse me, pardon me, I'm sorry to interrupt you, but I'm just curious; are you guys Muslims?" One of them said, "Yes," the second one said he was "undecided," the third wouldn't speak to me, and the fourth one said, "I'm a Darwinian evolutionist, a socialist, and a follower of Adolf Hitler." This guy was a Nazi!

Then, he started spouting off about all the "benefits" of socalism and being a Nazi! So, without even thinking (which is usually when I'm at my best) I got up, put on my coat, walked around the table and walked right up to him. My body language was open and non-aggressive. I leaned down just a little bit, and said,

"Excuse me, Sir, but there are three reasons why no man will stand before God with any excuse for ignoring or denying Him: The first reason is the universe and life itself. Psalm 19 says,

> The heavens declare the glory of God and the skies show his handiwork. Night after night they speak and there is no language where their voice is not heard.

"In other words, all a thinking person has to do is take a good look at the sun, the moon, the stars, the life-cycle of the planet we live on, and your own human body, which is fearfully and wonderfully made, to *know* that anything so complex, so perfectly designed and well balanced as is our world, there is no way all this could have made itself. The Bible says, 'The fool says in his heart there is no God!" I remember thinking to myself, did you just call this Nazi a fool?

"The second reason no man will stand before God with any excuse for ignoring or denying Him is: The word of God, living and written—that is Jesus Christ and the Bible. I can prove the Bible is true with one word—Israel.

"Thousands of years ago the Bible predicted that Israel would be destroyed as a nation, and the land would remain desolate for a long, long, time. And, in the last days Israel would come back as a nation.

"History proves that is exactly what happened. In A.D. 70, the Roman Empire destroyed Jerusalem and the Jews ran for their lives to the four corners of the Earth. The land remained desolate for almost 1,900 years!

"Then, after World War II when Hitler was finally stopped (I remember thinking to myself, did you just say that to this Nazi?), the Jews began to trickle back into the land. And, on May 14, 1948, Israel was recognized as a sovereign state by the United Nations, precisely as the Bible predicted! One of the reasons I'm a Christian is because I've read the Bible, and *nobody* can guess *that* good.

"Then we have the living Word, Jesus Christ. Jesus is the most famous Person who's ever lived. We live in the 21st century because 21 centuries ago a real, historical Person came to this planet who had such a profound impact on the world by what He said and did that the world marks time by His birth and His death. That's because three days after He was crucified, He raised Himself from the dead. Nobody ever did that before! Napoleon said of Jesus,

> I know men and I tell you that Jesus Christ is no mere man. Between Him and every other person there's no possible term of comparison. Caesar, Alexander, Charlemagne, and I have all founded empires, but on what did we base our genius? Upon force! Jesus Christ founded His empire on love, and today millions are willing to die for Him.

"The third reason no man will stand before God with any excuse for a ignoring or denying Him is written right inside your chest. I leaned down a little closer, lifted up my finger, pointed straight up, and said, Romans 2:15 says,

> *The law is written on every man's heart.*

"Every man from the beginning of time until the end of the world, whether he's ever seen a Bible or even heard of Jesus, knows in his heart it's wrong to murder, it's wrong to steal, it's wrong to lie, and it's wrong to have another man's wife. Every man knows there's a God in heaven because the sun, the moon, and the stars declare His glory. And, you know it's true, and I know you know it's true, and God knows you know it's true—isn't that true?"

He jumped out of his seat, held out his hand, smiling from ear to ear, and said, "Man, if I was going to choose a religion, I'd choose Christianity." And he shook my hand!

I said to my wife, "Honey, do you have the Muslim tracts? Give me the Muslim tracts!" (My wife has a purse as big as a suitcase with tracts for every situation—all in alphabetical order).

She pulled out four Muslim Gospel tracts and gave them to me. I offered one to each man and they each took it and said, "Thank you!" A few minutes later I went to pay our bill (and theirs) and left. What a blast that was! But, there's more.

EVERYBODY LOVES A HAPPY ENDING

A couple years later, I shared that story at a men's conference in Lakeland, Florida. After my message a man came up to me and said, "You're not going to believe this, but I just heard a man share his testimony at a church in Detroit. He said he was a former Nazi and some guy shared the Gospel with him in a Mexican restaurant in Chicago. It's gotta be you!"

Actually, I'm just a delivery boy. The credit goes to our great God and Savior the Lord Jesus Christ!

The only fear ordained by God is the fear of God and when you fear Him you don't fear anyone or anything—ever!

SMALL GROUP DISCUSSION QUESTIONS FOR CHAPTER NINE

1. Jesus said, "If you are ashamed of me before men I will be ashamed of you before my father in heaven." How does this verse make You feel? Why are so many people afraid of speaking up for Christ?
2. Why did Jesus send his disciples out in twos?
3. What are the advantages of having someone with you when you are in the world?
4. What was most meaningful to you in this chapter? Why?
5. What is idolatry?
6. What are the idols in your life? What are the idols in our nation?
7. Why does God hate idolatry?
8. Share a time when you did speak up for Jesus, or, share a time when you did not speak up for Jesus. How did it make you feel?
9. How do we get delivered from the fear of man?
10. What does God want you to do as a result of this chapter?

APPENDIX ONE

BUT WE'RE NOT UNDER LAW, WE'RE UNDER GRACE!

Before I say a word on this subject, you need to know that I know, we are saved by grace alone, through faith alone, through Christ alone, plus *nothing*. Our good works are the *result* of our salvation never the *cause* of it. Our justification is based on the fact that Christ satisfied the righteous demands of the law on our behalf.

Unfortunately, for many people, if you just mention the word "law," they go into something theologians call "hyperdispensationalism." Their immediate response is to recite Romans 6:14, completely out of context and blurt out…

> But we're not under law, we're under grace.

Whenever I hear that verse taken out of context, I like to ask, "Where does it say that in the Bible?" Almost always the response is something like, "I don't know, but it's in there somewhere."

Then I ask, "Well, what law is that verse referring to? Is it the law of God, the law of Moses, the Pentateuch (the first five books of the Bible), the entire Old Testament, the civil law, the ceremonial law, the moral law, the letter of the law, the spirit of the law, the dispensation of law, the law of condemnation and death written on tablets of stone, the perfect law of liberty, or the law of Christ?"

This is enough for most people to realize they do not understand the many facets of law in Scripture, which accounts for the confusion. Many people mistakenly believe that because the New Testament says "Christ fulfilled the law" that all law is obsolete and has no bearing on the life of a "New Testament Christian."

For those who might not understand the implications of taking a verse out of context, please refer back to chapter two. As for the verse at hand, first of all, the context of Romans 6 is about dying to sin (breaking the law), *not* grace nullifying the law.

Let's take a close look at one of the most frequently abused verses in the Bible, in context,

> *For sin shall not be master over you: for you are not under the Law, but under grace (Rom. 6:14).*

Can Paul mean, after all he has just said in chapter 6 about giving up sin (giving up breaking the law), that grace somehow nullifies the law? In light of Romans 3:31, that is an impossible argument,

> *Do we then nullify the law through faith? May it never be! On the contrary, we establish the law.*

How is it possible to believe that we are no longer under any obligation to obey God's moral law, since it is the law that defines what sin is? Romans 7:7 is crystal clear,

> *What shall we say then? Is the Law sin? May it never be! On the contrary, I would not have come to know sin except through the Law; for I would not have known about coveting if the Law had not said, "You shall not covet."*

To quote the second half of Romans 6:14 in an attempt to prove that the law is no longer relevant is to turn the verse around 180 degrees and make it say the exact opposite of what it means. It's not obeying the (moral) law that is forbidden, it's *breaking* the law we are supposed to give up! Look at the next two verses:

> *What then? Shall we sin (transgress the law) because we are not under Law but under grace? May it never be. Do you not know that when you present yourselves to someone as slaves for obedience, you are slaves of the one whom you obey, either of sin resulting in death, or of obedience resulting in righteousness?*

OBEDIENCE TO WHAT?

If you are a Christian, the word "slave" in verse 16 is your job title, and the word "obedience" is your job description. The question is, obedience to what? This verse is perfectly clear. You are either a slave to sin, or you are a slave to righteousness!

Apparently, many people now think since Jesus died on the cross it's okay for Christians to worship other gods or to bow down to statues. What about cursing using God's name? How many think God will just look the other way if we murder an *infidel*?

Does anyone in his right New Testament mind think God will just smile and wink if Christians decide it's alright to commit adultery or to marry more than one wife? What about stealing and lying? Are these transgressions now on the approved list since Christ made a way for us? Any takers for coveting against our neighbor?

If anything, the New Testament *raised* the standard. The Old Testament said, "Thou shalt not commit adultery," but the New Testament says, "If you even look upon a woman to lust after her, you have committed adultery already in your heart" (Matt. 5:27-28).

IF YOU'RE STILL NOT SURE, LET'S LOOK AT IT FROM ANOTHER POINT OF VIEW—WHAT IS THE MINISTRY OF GRACE?

The word "grace" in the Greek means not only unmerited favor, but, according to Spiros Zodhiates in the *Complete Word Study Dictionary of the New Testament*, grace "is initially regeneration, the work of the Holy Spirit in which spiritual life is given to man, and by which his nature is brought under the *dominion of righteousness*" (emphasis mine).[1] I love this one, James Strong said, "Grace is the divine influence upon the heart, and its reflection in the life, including gratitude."

TITUS 2:11-12

For the grace of God has appeared, bringing salvation [i.e., deliverance] to all men, instructing us to deny ungodliness and worldly desires and to live sensibly, righteously and godly in the present age, looking for the blessed hope and the appearing of the glory of our great God and Savior, Christ Jesus; who gave Himself for us, that He might redeem us from every lawless deed and purify for Himself a people for His own possession, zealous for good deeds (italics mine).

Look at what Paul says in the very next chapter of Romans,

THEREFORE THE LAW IS HOLY, AND THE COMMANDMENT IS HOLY AND JUST AND GOOD–ROMANS 7:12

Why would Paul use the present-tense verb *is* if the Law did not have spiritual relevance to his readers? Does Paul say the Law *was* holy, the commandment *was* holy, the Law *was* just and good?

FOR WE KNOW THAT THE LAW IS SPIRITUAL–ROMANS 7:14

The understanding of what is meant by "the law is spiritual" is defined for us by Jesus in Matthew 5. Jesus equates the physical act of murder (the letter of the law) with unforgiveness which is the spirit of the law. Jesus equates adultery (the letter) with lust (the spiritual). The physical can be seen by men, but the spiritual is a condition of the heart, which only God can see (1 Sam. 16:7).

So, how do we correctly interpret verses like…

FOR CHRIST IS THE END OF THE LAW FOR RIGHTEOUSNESS TO EVERYONE WHO BELIEVES–ROMANS 10:4

Please remember, the New Testament was originally written in Greek not English. The word *end* would have been better translated as *aim* or *goal*! This is found in the margins of many study Bibles. Christ is the goal of the law. For all practical purposes, virtually everything in the Old Testament pointed to Jesus. This does not mean, however, that we are now exempt from obedience to God's moral law. On the contrary, holy obedience is the highest form of worship!

> *I urge you therefore, brethren, by the mercies of God, to present your bodies a living and holy sacrifice, acceptable to God, which is your spiritual service of worship (Rom. 12:1).*

FOR THROUGH THE LAW I DIED TO THE LAW, THAT I MIGHT LIVE TO GOD–GALATIANS 2:19

It was the Law that showed Paul he could never be saved by keeping the Law! He died to the idea of trying to be *saved* by obeying it. The Law showed him he was a sinner and that he needed God's grace. That is the most valuable and precious truth any human being could ever know (Gal. 3:24)!

YOU HAVE BEEN SEVERED FROM CHRIST, YOU WHO ARE SEEKING TO BE JUSTIFIED BY THE LAW; YOU HAVE FALLEN FROM GRACE—GALATIANS 5:4

When a person seeks to be justified (saved) by keeping the law, it is that very law that will condemn him. For the Christian, the Ten Commandments represent practical holiness—not justification by works! For the non-Christian, that same law is his death sentence. You are either under law, or you are under grace.

HAVING ABOLISHED IN HIS FLESH THE ENMITY, THAT IS, THE LAW OF COMMANDMENTS CONTAINED IN ORDINANCES, SO AS TO CREATE IN HIMSELF ONE NEW MAN FROM THE TWO, THUS MAKING PEACE—EPHESIANS 2:15

"Through his death, Christ abolished OT ceremonial laws, feasts, and sacrifices which uniquely separated the Jews from gentiles. God's moral law (as summarized in the Ten Commandments and written on the hearts of all men, Rom. 2:15) was not abolished but subsumed in the New Covenant, however, because it reflects his own holy nature."—John MacArthur Study Bible

DO WE THEN MAKE VOID THE LAW THROUGH FAITH? CERTAINLY NOT! ON THE CONTRARY, WE ESTABLISH THE LAW—ROMANS 3:31

Now that we live in the dispensation of grace, is the law obsolete? No. On the contrary, the reason we need grace is because we have broken God's law. Grace presupposes law.

There is nothing in the course of mankind's history, nothing in the universe that so established, upheld, or confirmed the validity of the law as when the wrath of God was poured out on the sinless Lamb of God on the cross of Calvary. But, its work continues. Since the beginning of time, every man, woman, and child that has ever been born has died (with the exception of Enoch and Elijah). Death is the result of sin, and "sin is the transgression of the law" (1 Jn. 3:4 KJV). Every time someone dies, every death proves that the law is still in effect and still being enforced. The law says that if you sin, you shall surely die (see Rom. 6:23, Gen. 2:17). Just as death presupposes life, so grace presupposes law.

FOR THE LAW OF THE SPIRIT OF LIFE IN CHRIST JESUS HAS SET YOU FREE FROM THE LAW OF SIN AND DEATH–ROMANS 8:2

How can the Ten Commandments, referred to as "the law of sin and death" in 2 corinthians 3:9, also be called "the perfect law of liberty" in James 1:25 and 2:10? The answer is simple. The law, like a coin, has two sides: On one side it defines holiness, and on the other it defines sin. When God says, "Thou shalt not lie" (a sin), He is by implication saying, "Thou shall tell the truth" (holiness and freedom).

Whenever God says "no" to one thing, He is saying "yes" to something better! The law of sin and death in 2 Corinthians 3 is also the perfect law of liberty in James 2. It all depends on which side of the cross you're on. The same law that once condemned me before I was a Christian, now points me to holiness. This verse (Rom. 8:2) sets me free from the condemnation of the law, not my obligation, based on love, to obey it!

H.A. Ironside, ". . . that law, so terrible to the sinner, is a law of liberty to the regenerated one, because it commands the very behavior in which the one born of God finds his joy and delight."

John Wesley, "Therefore I cannot spare the Law one moment, no more than I can spare Christ, seeing I now want it as much to keep me to Christ, as I ever wanted it to bring me to Him. Otherwise this 'evil heart of unbelief' would immediately 'depart from the living God.' Indeed each is continually sending me to the other—the Law to Christ, and Christ to the Law."

Martin Luther, "The law and the Gospel are given to the end that we may learn to know both how guilty we are, and to what again we should return."

The Apostle Paul, "What shall we say then? Shall we continue in sin (*break the law*) that grace may abound? Certainly not! How shall we who died to sin live any longer in it?" (*Italics mine*).

Jesus Christ, "And Jesus said to her, 'Neither do I condemn you; go and sin no more (John 8:10-11).'"

So, what does, "Go and sin no more" mean?

APPENDIX TWO

SATAN'S MASTER PLAN OF EVANGELISM AND THE IMMORAL MAJORITY

The number one deception in our world is the same lie that Satan used with Adam and Eve when he said, "You surely shall not die."

Many, if not most, of the people I witness to are deceived into thinking that God will not reject them because they are basically "good people." After all, they reason, "I'm a good person; I've never murdered anyone."

The problem with that line of "reasoning" is that we humans are not the ones who define what "good" is. Scripture says, "Only God is good" (Matt. 19:17). God alone is perfect, and is therefore the only One qualified and capable of establishing and enforcing an absolute, universal standard of righteousness and truth for all people.

GOING TO CHURCH DOESN'T MAKE YOU A CHRISTIAN, ANY MORE THAN EATING AT MCDONALD'S MAKES YOU A HAMBURGER.

Sadly, there are many people who think they are Christians simply because they "believe in God" and go to church. Since many people who attend church regularly do not study their Bibles firsthand, they end up getting their "daily bread" only once a week. To compound the problem, many of these weekly feedings are served by pastors who, by and large, are not serious students of the Bible themselves!

Consequently, the stuff they serve is often stale, secondhand, and boring. It's one thing to read the Bible and come up with a few "appropriate comments" for Sunday morning, it's another thing to seriously study the Word of God in order to live and teach with results. It's one thing to come up with something to say because you are having a meeting, it's quite another to have a meeting because you have something to say.

For the worldly minded minister, there is little or no incentive to preach the whole counsel of God, since to do so could be offensive. This would hurt attendance, which means giving would decline, which could cost the pastor his job. This is why so much of the church looks more like a social club on a cruise ship to heaven, rather than a battleship, armed and ready to storm the gates of hell. The attitude of many church goers (and preachers) is that it's okay to have church on Sunday, as long as it doesn't interfere with lunch or the game. The end product is a church that is, for the most part, indistinguishable from the world. The word church (ekklesia), means: an assembly of God's people, called *out* from the world.

GEORGE GALLUP

"Most Americans who profess Christianity don't know the basic teachings of the faith, and they don't act significantly different from non-Christians in their daily lives. Over all, the Sunday school and religious education system in this country is not working. Not being grounded in the faith, these professing believers are open for anything that comes along. Studies show that new age beliefs for example, are just as strong among traditionally religious people as among those who are not traditionally religious. And the churched are just as likely as the unchurched to engage in unethical behavior. The studies also show a growing percentage of Christians believe they can sustain their faith without going to church."

BIBLICAL ILLITERACY IS OFF THE CHARTS

I recently heard a former Jehovah's (False) Witness on the radio explain how he knocked on doors for six years, and not once in all that time did he meet a Christian who could refute his "errors" using a Bible!

In another instance, I heard a missionary tell about a legalistic Christian congregation in Africa. He almost seemed to be bragging as he said, "Some of our people have almost been stoned for preaching grace." When a man thinks he can be saved by "being good enough," you don't keep preaching grace. His problem is, he doesn't understand the law (Rom. 3:20).

I have actually heard Christian leaders say things like, "There is no law in the New Testament." Friend, you can't even play Tiddley Winks without rules. Apparently, these men fail to distinguish between the civil, the ceremonial, and the moral law. Romans 3:20; 31, and 7:7 make it abundantly clear, God's definition of sin has never changed.

NO SUCH THING AS A GOOD EXCUSE

Ever since the Garden of Eden, man has gone to great lengths to avoid, deny, ignore, suppress, or redefine the doctrine of sin. One artful dodge is to call it crime. In this case, we are no longer breaking God's law, but man's. This shifts the responsibility from the church to the state.

Today we refer to alcoholism and drug addition as a disease rather than a moral weakness. You can't repent of a disease. Homosexuality (an abomination to God) is now called a "preexisting genetic condition." Nothing to be sorry for here, it's perfectly natural, right? Wrong! Otherwise, God would have been unjust in destroying Sodom and Gomorrah. There seems to be no end to man's shell-game with words.

Today we have no-fault divorce, no-fault insurance, and a woman's "right to choose." We blame everybody and everything except the real culprit. When God confronted Adam about his transgression in the Garden of Eden, Adam turned right around and said, "It was the woman who did it and you're the one who gave her to me!"

NOTES

CHAPTER 1: THE GREATEST DEMONSTRATION OF POWER ANYONE HAS EVER SEEN
1. Bob Cornuke, *Discovering the Real Mt. Sinai,* Video.
2. Hebert Lockyer, *All the Miracles of the Bible (*Grand Rapids: Zondervon Books, 1961), 70.

CHAPTER 2: THE BIBLE'S BIG PICTURE
1. Sidney Greidanus, *Preaching Christ from the Old Testament (*Grand Rapids: Eerdmans Publishing Co. 1999).

CHAPTER 3: THE LAW IS WRITTEN ON EVERY MAN'S HEART
1. From an article entitled: "Confessions of a Professed Atheist," *Report: Perspective on the News,* Vol. 3 (June 1966), p.19.
2. I am indebted to Lakita Garth for this excellent illustration on purity.
3. Lee Strobel, live interview on *Midday Connection,* WMBI FM radio, Chicago, Nov. 29, 2000.

CHAPTER 4: GOD'S MASTER PLAN OF SALVATION
1. J. C. Ryle, *Holiness* (Darlington: Evangelical Press, 1879, 1995), 1.
2. Keith Green, *What's Wrong with the Modern Gospel* (Lindale: Last Days Ministries, 1981), 2.
3. Ravi Zacharias, *Let My People Think* Radio program.

CHAPTER 5: HOW TO PRESENT THE GOSPEL THE WAY JESUS DID
1. Comfort, Ibid.

CHAPTER 6: IS THIS REALLY NEW TESTAMENT THEOLOGY?
1. Warren Wiersbe, *The Bible Exposition Commentary* (Wheaton: Victor Books, 1989).
2. Ibid., 72.
3. Ibid., 250.
4. A.C. Gaebelein, *The Gospel of Matthew* (New York: Our Hope, 1910), 104.
5. Arthur W. Pink, *Exposition of the Gospel of John* (Grand Rapids: Zondervan, 1975), 106.
6. Leon Morris, *The Gospel According to John* (Grand Rapids: William B. Eerdmans, 1995), 295.
7. Matthew Henry, *The Bethany Parallel Commentary New Testament* (Minneapolis: Bethany House, 1983), 453.
8. Charles Finney, Ray Comfort, *The 10 Cannons of God's Law,* Oak Brook: Institute in Basic Life Principles, 1992, Video.

CHAPTER 7: DON'T TAKE MY WORD FOR IT
1. C.H. Spurgeon, *Lectures to My Students* (Grand Rapids: Zondervan, 1954), 338.
2. John Calvin, *Institutes of the Christian Religion.*
3. John Wesley, *The Works of John Wesley, vols. 5–6 (*Grand Rapids: Baker Books, 1991), 449.
4. Ray Comfort, *The Ten Cannons of God's Law,* Video.
5. Ibid.
6. Idem., Matthew Henry.
8. Comfort Ibid.
9. Augustine, *Concerning the Letter and the Spirit.*
10. Jonathan Edwards, John MacArthur Jr., *The Vanishing Conscience* (Dallas: Word, 1994), 245.
11. Spurgeon Ibid.
12. Idem., Wesley, 445.

13. Martin Luther.
14. General William Booth.
15. Arthur W. Pink, *The Ten Commandments* (Grand Rapids: Baker Books, 1976), 14.
16. H. A. Ironside, *Hebrews, James, Peter* (Neptune: Loizeaux Brothers, Inc., 1947, 82), 21.
17. Idem., Leon Morris.
18. Walter Kaiser, *Toward an Exegetical Theology (Grand Rapids: Baker* Books, 1981).
19. John MacArthur Jr., *The Gospel According to Jesus* (Grand Rapids: Zondervan, 1988), 84.
20. Michael Horton, *The Law of Perfect Freedom* (Chicago: Moody Press, 1993), 36.
21. Kay Arthur, *Beloved,* (1994).
22. Alexander Maclaren, *Expositions of Holy Scripture* (Grand Rapids: Baker Books, 1974), 46.
23. Donald Grey Barnhouse, *Romans, Vol. I* (Grand Rapids: Eerdmans, 1952), 275.
24. Jamieson, Fausset, Brown, *The Bethany Parallel Commentary on the New Testament* (Minneapolis: Bethany House, 1983), 898.
25. D. Martyn Lloyd-Jones, *Romans, Atonement & Justification* (Grand Rapids: Zondervan, 1989), 21.
26. Idem., Maclaren, 98.
27. Gleason Archer, *A Survey of Old Testament Introduction* (Chicago: Moody Press, 1964), 253.
28. R.C. Sproul, [audio tape], used by permission.
29. Class lecture, Trinity Evangelical Divinity School, Deerfield, Illinois,. 1994, D A. Carson, used by permission.
30. Erwin Lutzer.
31. Erwin Lutzer, Moody Memorial Church, Chicago, Personal Interview, 1993.
32. Noah Webster, *The 1828 American Dictionary of the English Language* (San Francisco: Foundation for American Christian Education).

CHAPTER 8: THE PERFECT LAW OF LIBERTY

1. William Barclay, *The Letters of James and Peter* (Philadelphia: Westminster Press, 1976), 60.
2. Idem., Ravi Zacharias.
3. Ibid.
4. Idem., Henry, 916.

CHAPTER 10: THE FEAR OF MAN VS. THE FEAR OF GOD

1. A.W. Tozer, *The Best of A.W. Tozer* (Grand Rapids: Baker Books, 1978), 177.
2. A.W. Tozer, *The Knowledge of the Holy* (New York, NY: Harper Collins, 1961,) 1.

APPENDIX ONE: WE'RE NOT UNDER LAW, WE'RE UNDER GRACE

1. Spiros Zodhiates, *Complete Word Study Dictionary: New Testament* (Chattanooga: AMG, 1993), 1469.
2. Gleason Archer, *A Survey of Old Testament Introduction* (Chicago: Moody Press, 1964), 253.
3. Ironside, Ibid.

APPENDIX TWO: SATAN'S MASTER PLAN OF EVANGELISM AND THE IMMORAL MAJORITY

1. *National and International Religion Report, Vol. 5, No.11* (Washington D.C.: Media Management, 1991), 1.

For more resources visit our websites:
Voice-wilderness.org
Gal416.org